The Art and Business of Online Writing

How to Beat the Game of Capturing and Keeping Attention

Nicolas Cole

"My articles have been read by over 100M people. Cole's articles have been read more than mine, and I can personally attest this book will teach you everything you need to know to reach millions of people with your writing."

—DR. BENJAMIN HARDY,
bestselling author of *Personality Isn't Permanent*

This book is dedicated to anyone who wants to become a professional writer on their own terms.

I wish someone had gifted me this book when I was 23 years old, graduating from Columbia College Chicago with a degree in creative writing.

Enjoy.

Table of Contents

The Art and Business of Online Writing

DiFf
PUBLISHING

Logging In (Introduction)

The Game Of Online Writing

Writing online is a game.

I first started playing the game in 2007. I was 17 years old, a junior in high school, and one of the top World of Warcraft players in North America. Long gone were the days of the internet only being used by forward-thinking entrepreneurs and computer scientists. The social digital revolution had begun: Facebook was three years old, YouTube was two, and Twitter was a newborn wailing at the top of its lungs.

Right before school let out for the summer, this new website emerged in the competitive gaming community, called GameRiot. It was a "social media" site for gamers—before the term "social media" had even become part of the world's vocabulary. I'd heard about the site from a gaming blogger I loved reading. Every morning before school, I would wake up, make myself two eggs on toast (wheat), and read his latest blog. He was one of the few top-tier gamers who actually had his own website, so when he made a post one morning saying he was going to start writing somewhere else instead, I knew to pay attention.

While the rest of my family played in the pool in the backyard, I was upstairs in my bedroom. With freezing cold air blasting out of the air conditioner above my head, I sat at my desk hunched over my keyboard with my face three inches from my monitor, exploring GameRiot.

I was staring at one of the internet's first "social blogs," exclusively for gamers.

Similar to the way a Facebook or Twitter feed looked, the center of the website was an infinite scrolling feed of posts. Catering to the "gamer" mentality, in the upper right-hand corner there was a leaderboard of the Top 10 most popular blogs on the site—and sure enough, sitting at #1, was a recent post by my favorite gaming blogger, Ming.

I decided, right then and there, I was going to become a competitive blogger too.

The reason I didn't start a website of my own was because I didn't know how.

In the mid 2000s, there were no website templates, no easy-to-use graphic design tools, no one-click solutions. Almost everything had to be custom designed and coded. And since I had no money, I couldn't afford to hire someone to help me.

But on this new site for gamers, all of that was taken care of.

When you created your own profile, you could easily upload a photo and write a short bio. You could browse other people's posts on the front page. You could scroll through different topics. You could comment, and other people could comment back to you. The whole website was a game, no different to me than the World of Warcraft—and without thinking twice about it, I decided I was going to start writing there too.

Every night, after playing 3v3 against some of the top gamers in the world, I would close the World of Warcraft and write that night's blog post. At first, I tried to make my blog the go-to resource for high-level gameplay information, breaking down team compositions, winning strategies, and little tricks to give gamers a competitive edge. But over time, I started to realize it wasn't the informative stuff that made the front page—it was drama.

Gamers loved knowing which teams had rivalries with who, which players had lost their shit after a loss, and who had been sneaky enough to capture an audio recording of the outburst for the entire World of Warcraft community to hear. More importantly, they wanted to know what some of the best players were like *in real life.*

It didn't take me long to realize that readers didn't just want to learn how to be better gamers themselves.

They also wanted to be entertained.

Watching Ming execute this strategy perfectly, I began to mirror my writing style off his. Every one of his posts was a blend between informative content and controversy-inducing tangents. In one single paragraph, he would go from explaining the inner workings of the Rogue class to venting about how his Asian parents had arranged his upcoming marriage and the whole event was getting in the way of his 3v3 team making it to BlizzCon's first ever Arena World Championship Tournament. The comment section of his posts would explode with gamers either curiously wanting to know more about his love life, or ridiculing him for thinking the World of Warcraft was more important than his wedding day.

This is what made Ming the #1 most-read writer on the site week after week, month after month.

Everything changed for me when I started incorporating more of my real life into my writing.

I wrote about how my parents, my teachers, even my peers at high school didn't respect video games—but for some reason enthusiastically supported football, basketball, and other organized sports.

I wrote about organized education, and how as long as the internet continued to develop, I continued to lose faith in there being a real need to attend college.

I even wrote about the most popular girl in school, a brunette cheerleader, and how there was one week of my high school career where a series of unfathomable events unfolded: I went to my very first high school party ever; word got out that I was one of the top World of Warcraft players in the country; the hottest girl in our school professed her love to me; we went on a date; kissed; rumors started flying we were dating; I catapulted from the bottom of the social totem pole to the absolute peak; then she started getting made fun of for liking me; she denied anything ever happened; then she made up reverse rumors about how I was obsessed with her and probably a stalker; and by the end of the week, I was right back to sitting by myself during lunch—except this time, with threats coming from the entire baseball team that if I ever talked to her again, I'd get my head bashed in with a baseball bat.

All of which was true.

As a result, I instantly became one of the most popular writers on the site.

And by the time I took a seat in my first journalism class at the University of Missouri, one year later, I was one of the most-read gaming writers on the internet.

"The internet is a fad, blogging is a trend, and real journalism will never die," my college professor said.

At the bottom of a sea of 500 students, my Intro to Journalism professor stood on a wooden stage and paced back and forth with a microphone in his hand. I was sitting in the very back row. Every single student below me and around me was wearing black and yellow, the school's colors, with a silver MacBook Pro in front of them and Facebook on their screen. I was wearing a brown hoodie, refreshing my gaming blog.

"The only way anyone could possibly be seen as a credible writer on the internet," he said, "was if they had more than 10,000 readers on their blog."

The class laughed out loud—not because they thought he was wrong, but because they agreed with him.

10,000 daily readers seemed impossible in 2008.

I raised my hand.

"I don't think the internet is a trend," I said. Every single student in the auditorium rustled in their seats to look at me.

"Then I suppose you have 10,000 readers on your blog too?" the professor said, chuckling into his microphone, assuming that would stop the conversation right then and there. The only people who had that sort of web traffic were columnists at major publications.

I raised my hand again. Not waiting to be called on, I said, "Yea, I do."

My teacher didn't believe me, which was fine because I didn't believe him either. I couldn't imagine a future that didn't involve the internet. Blogging was only the beginning. And if he truly thought print journalism was never going to die, then I was in the wrong major.

I didn't show up to that class for the rest of the semester, and transferred schools the very next year.

I moved back to Chicago to study creative writing.

Many of the key lessons I learned about Online Writing as a teenager wouldn't become conscious until almost seven years later.

My journey to becoming one of the most-read writers on the internet truly started when I graduated from Columbia College Chicago with a degree in fiction writing.

I had just started working at a local advertising agency as an entry-level copywriter. For the first time in my life, I started to learn what it actually meant to "build a brand." Terms like *exposure, audience, engagement,* gave me a language for many of the things I had intuitively understood as a teenage gamer, but never knew what to call them. I didn't know that 10,000 people reading my blog every day made me "an influencer." I didn't realize that hundreds of thousands of views equated to "brand exposure," or that the thirty, forty, fifty comments on every single one of my posts meant I had a higher "engagement rate" than other bloggers.

I had tried starting a blog during college, called *Nothin' But A Notepad*, but it was largely unsuccessful. I never once surpassed more than 100 views on any of my posts. I was using a standard blogging platform, called Blogger, and even had my own profile and URL. I could customize the color of the header and a few of the design elements. But it was missing the most important piece of the puzzle: there was no social component, no way for readers to explore and discover new, interesting writers. And without this discovery feature, the likelihood of someone coming across my blog was slim to none.

There was no "game."

As soon as I graduated from college, I found myself daydreaming in the middle of the work day as to how I was going to "make it" as a writer. I decided to text a gamer friend of mine and ask his opinion on where I should start writing online. He was a professional World of Warcraft player and YouTuber with a few hundred thousand subscribers, and was extremely savvy when it came to understanding how to capture and keep people's attention.

"If gamers and vloggers have YouTube, and fitness models and fashionistas have Instagram, where should writers, write?" I asked.

It wasn't really Facebook. And it wasn't really Twitter.

"You should take a look at Quora," he said.

I'd never heard of it.

On the surface, Quora was a cleaner looking version of Yahoo! Answers—the weirdly honest Question/Answer site that felt more like an anonymous, user-generated WebMD than the "knowledge market" it claimed to be. On Quora, however, anyone could ask a question, and anyone could write an answer—but all the highest-performing answers were written from credible, engaging, articulate people. The questions ranged from, "What's it like to be in the courtroom with a convicted murderer?" to "How do I lose weight?"

For the rest of the afternoon, and the rest of the week, and ultimately the rest of the month, all I did was read answers on Quora. My feed was filled with a never-ending stream of questions—and attached to them, answers written like short stories. That's what hooked me. Someone would ask the question, "What's it like to be a serial entrepreneur?" and the most popular answer wasn't a formal definition of entrepreneurship. It was an answer that started with, "When I was 20 years old, I sold my first company for a million dollars." And before I could even decide whether or not I wanted to keep reading the thing in front of me, I was already flying through the second paragraph, dying to know what happened next.

Every single question on Quora was a creative writing prompt.

At least, that's the way I saw it.

The most popular answers, the ones with the most views, upvotes, and comments, weren't "answers," as much as they were *stories*. And the people with the most followers weren't celebrities, but natural-born storytellers. They would turn the question, "What do you regret most in life?" into a nostalgic retelling of getting married too young. They would transform, "Does mustard go with chicken?" into an analytical thinkpiece you would be more accustomed to finding in *The New Yorker*. Even questions like, "How do you build a successful enterprise business?" became public post-mortems by wise investors, sharing war stories of promising startups turned catastrophic failures.

I had the very same reaction to Quora as I did that old gaming website where I'd started my very first blog.

"I can do this," I thought. "I can beat this game."

At 24 years old, I was far from being an industry professional or public figure worthy of enlightening the masses with my wisdom. But there were questions on Quora I felt comfortable answering based solely on my experiences in life thus far.

For example, I had learned a lot about the importance of building positive habits living the life of a bodybuilder throughout college.

I had learned some hard lessons about life in my early 20s overcoming substance abuse issues, and going stone-cold sober from ages 21 to 26.

I had unconventional opinions on the positive impact of video games after my teenage years spent being a competitive gamer.

And I had been writing online long enough to know a thing or two about online writing.

I didn't need to be an "expert" to answer those types of questions.

I just needed to share my story.

For an entire year straight, I challenged myself to write one Quora answer, every single day.

I knew that if I wanted to be successful on Quora, then I needed to treat it the same way I had treated writing online as a teenager. Worst case scenario, I'd spend a year practicing my writing. Best case, I'd build an audience and jumpstart my career.

The questions I chose were ones I felt "qualified" to answer—as in, I had some sort of "achievement" I could point to for credibility. For example, the very first question I answered on Quora was, "Is Elite Daily a legitimate site? Why?" The reason I chose to answer that question was because, a few years prior, I had actually been one of the first writers on Elite Daily when they first opened the site to outside contributors. I thought, with that small detail as my "credibility," people would want to hear what I had to say.

My first Quora answer received a whopping 37 views.

Now, this is where most people would have given up. Notoriously, human beings spend an awful lot of time imagining the big achievement we want for ourselves at the end of the journey, but struggle tremendously getting through the beginning—where we suck.

Gamers, on the other hand, know that you have to play Level 1 over and over again in order to reach Level 2. And then you have to play Level 2 over and over again before you can reach Level 3. And if you can just keep on keeping on your journey, learning and mastering each level, you will eventually climb all the way to the top of the ladder.

That's how you "beat the game."

Unphased by my first answer's performance, I pressed on.

The next answer I wrote was to the question, "Should I take a job as an Executive Assistant?"

Earlier that day, the creative director and one of the Managing Directors of the agency I was working at had gotten frustrated and said out loud, "So many things are falling through the cracks. I need someone to follow me around with a pooper scooper. I need an assistant." The other nine people around the table looked down at their computers, hoping to hide from being chosen for the job.

Without hesitation, I said, "I'll do it."

Everyone looked at me like I was crazy. But I knew exactly what I was doing.

The guy was brilliant. And I didn't care if my job title was

Professional Pooper Scooper. I knew that by getting closer to him, we'd be forced to spend more time together. And since I wanted him to be my mentor, answering emails and monitoring his calendar were a small price to pay in exchange for all the knowledge I'd receive in return.

"Done," he said. "Come with me. We're going to go land some new clients."

I followed him into the next room. He pushed his laptop in front of me, handing over his personal inbox, and said, "Let's start with an email to Jamie." He then paced around the office while dictating an email for me to type to one of his former classmates from the University of Chicago Booth School of Business—an executive at a publicly-traded company.

After two hours had passed, dozens of emails had been sent, and the day was done, I packed up my laptop, walked to the Starbucks down the street on the way to the train station, and answered that question, "Should I take a job as an Executive Assistant?"

In three short paragraphs, as if reflecting on the day in my journal, I explained the logic behind the decision to sign myself up for an assistant job that didn't pay me anything extra.

Here's what I wrote:

> *This is more of a question of whether or not the person you are assisting is worth your efforts.*
>
> *If they are a master of their domain, then simply sitting in the same room as them will inevitably rub off on you in ways that are impossible to quantify on a sheet*

of paper detailing job experience—especially if it is in a field where they will be conversing/communicating with high-profile clients.

Being the assistant to someone in that position allows you to see parts of an industry you wouldn't otherwise have access to. Think about it this way: how many years would you have to invest before they let you sit in on a meeting with a high-profile client? If you're their assistant, you're immediately allowed access (pending situation, of course).

If this is NOT going to be the case, and you will be nothing more than answering phones and regurgitating emails, I'd suggest looking elsewhere. But the opportunity to work closely with someone in a successful position most often translates into some sort of mentorship—an invaluable opportunity that will end up cultivating more important parts of yourself (confidence, business savviness, professionalism, etc.) than other simpler task-oriented skills.

That post got more than 1,000 views.

I was trending in the right direction.

Over the months that followed, I started to create a routine around taking whatever I had learned that day at work and using it as inspiration for my writing on Quora. Less worried about whether or not I was the most credible person to be answering each question, I focused all of my energy into making my answer the most relatable to whoever was experiencing (or wanted to experience) similar things in life. I tried to think about exactly *when* I had learned the answer to each question, what had happened, what was said to me, when it had "clicked," and then shared that.

I didn't need to be an expert on the topic. I just needed to be self-aware enough to verbalize how, where, and when I had learned that lesson, too.

As a result, my writing exploded. By the end of 2014, my first year writing on Quora, I had accumulated more than 3,000,000 views.

Day in, and day out, I showed up to work, spent all day playing Executive Assistant soaking up knowledge from my newfound mentor, and then would walk to the Starbucks down the street after work to write on Quora. I'd combine whatever I'd learned that day with the larger life lessons I'd learned as a pro gamer, or bodybuilder, and write my answer. The more answers I wrote, the more I learned what topics were resonating with the most people, and the more I started to realize what people really enjoyed about my writing.

This was exactly the same lesson I'd learned as a teenage gaming blogger: when I wrote about niche topics, viewership was mediocre.

But when I wrote about universal life lessons, my writing went viral.

January, 2015, I landed on the front page of Reddit.

As most stories like this go, I really didn't want to write anything that day.

Work was starting to get more demanding. I was staying

at the office later and later. But I was seeing success writing every day on Quora, and told myself these were the moments that defined how seriously I wanted to become a professional writer.

Did I want it bad enough?

Before I left the office that day, I opened up Quora and scrolled through my feed to find a question I could answer quickly. It didn't need to be a masterpiece—just something so I could say, "I accomplished my goal today." A few seconds later, my eye caught the question, "Is it possible to change so much you no longer recognize yourself?"

In less than ten minutes, I rattled off a quick response. Three paragraphs, nothing fancy. At the top, I placed a before and after photo: on the left, me as a skinny teenager with an S-curved spine and a concave chest, and on the right, me at 25 years old, 180 pounds, completely shredded.

I wrote about what it was like to be that kid on the left. How I felt sick almost every day of my entire adolescence (undiagnosed with Celiac disease). How I was a straight C student, didn't have many friends, and the ones I did have lived in my computer and gaming headset. How I was lonely and depressed, thought often about committing suicide, and couldn't wait for the day I left for college.

In the next paragraph, I wrote about what life was like being that guy on the right. How I had graduated college at the top of my class with a near-perfect GPA. How I had made friends with the "big guys" at the gym and joined their inner circle of bodybuilders and powerlifters. How I had started meditating, gotten a job in advertising, and barely remembered that kid on the left—skinny, awkward, and alone.

I hit publish on the post, packed up my backpack, and walked to the train.

By the time I got back to my apartment, forty-five minutes later, one of my roommates at the time found me in the kitchen and said, "Dude, did you know you're on the front page of Reddit right now?"

My short, three-paragraph post had gone massively viral. Every time I refreshed my Quora profile, I had another few hundred followers and another ten thousand views on the post. By the end of the night, it had crossed more than 300,000 views. And by the end of the week, it had reached 1,000,000.

That's when I launched www.nicolascole.com

Knowing I had a limited window of time to capitalize, I spent that entire weekend putting together a personal website.

Not because I wanted to start writing there—but because I now had a product to sell.

While my Quora answer continued accumulating hundreds of thousands of views, my inbox was exploding with people all asking the same questions: "How did you transform your body? What's your workout routine? What's your diet like? How many days per week do you go to the gym? How did you put on muscle as an ectomorph?"

As fast as I could, I wrote two eBooks: one with all my favorite workout routines, and another with my exact meal plan. I called the series, "Skinny to Shredded," sticking with the before and after photo that had now sparked a massive debate on Reddit as to whether or not I was "juicing" (I've never taken steroids, for the record). I designed the eBooks myself. I watched tutorial video after tutorial video trying to figure out how to create a digital store on my new website. And come Monday morning, the following week, I launched my personal website and first two eBooks.

I was, technically, an "author."

My phone buzzed in my pocket every time someone bought a copy.

Sitting in our Monday morning team meeting at work, I looked at my phone under the table and saw another string of Stripe notifications. My answer was still going viral on Quora, so I'd edited the original post to include a link to my new eBooks at the bottom.

This was how I made my first $2,000 as a writer, and as an entrepreneur.

Knowing this wouldn't last forever, I tried very hard not to let myself get attached to the success of that one article. The likelihood of my next Quora answer landing on the front page of Reddit was close to none, so as soon as the traffic began to die down, I went back to practicing the basics. I stuck with my habit of writing an answer per day, every day—and even though I never wrote another answer quite as viral as that one, consistency is what kept me growing, growing, growing.

A few weeks later, I had my first answer republished in *Inc Magazine*: "In what ways do you work smarter, rather than harder?"

A month after that, *The Huffington Post.*

And then *TIME. Business Insider. Fortune. Forbes.*

From June to the end of the year, I was averaging more than 500,000 organic views on my writing every single month, with at least one of my answers being republished by a major publication every single week. In November, when Quora announced their list of Top Writers for the year, one of their moderators sent me a message letting me know I'd been selected—and that I had set a new record for being the fastest user to go from creating an account on the platform to becoming a Top Writer. In addition, my answer to the question, "Should we ban World of Warcraft since so many teenagers have had their lives ruined?" was going to be republished in Quora's print anthology (a compilation of the platform's most unique works for that year, in print form).

By the end of 2015, I had become the #1 most-read writer on all of Quora.

As a way of bringing the platform's Top Writers together, Quora hosted a Top Writer conference in New York City every December—and this year, I was invited.

The only problem was, I couldn't really afford to go. Only two years out of college, I was making slightly more than minimum wage as a copywriter, and a single day trip to New York would wipe out all of my savings. Luckily, my boss and mentor had taken an interest in my obsession with Quora, wondering how I'd been able to accumulate more than 5,000,000 views on my writing while the agency's website blog could barely get more than 50 views per post. He had spent the majority of his 20s and early 30s living in New York, said it was the best city on earth, and offered to take me there for a long weekend so I could attend the conference.

"You have to go," he said. "You earned it."

A few weeks later, I walked into the low-lit restaurant in New York and introduced myself as "Nicolas Cole." This was the first time I'd ever said my pen name out loud.

Immediately, the girl behind the makeshift check-in desk recognized me and said, "You came! We were hoping you'd make it. You've caused quite a storm on Quora this year." After she handed me my nametag, Quora's Head of Global Writer Relations pulled me aside and said, "Hey, great to meet you in person." I knew his name because he was the one who had messaged me about my becoming a Top Writer on the platform.

"I'm not supposed to tell you this," he said, "but we have some internal metrics we look at and I thought you should know. You are the most-read writer on our entire site."

In 2015, Quora had more than 200,000,000 users.

Attending the Top Writer conference in New York changed my life.

I got to meet some of the other Top Writers on the platform, including James Altucher (author of WSJ best-seller *Choose Yourself*), David S. Rose (founder of New York Angels and CEO of Gust), and dozens more. I got to meet a few people from Quora's syndication team, who managed the relationships between Quora and all the major publications that had been syndicating my work. I even had a handful of other Top Writers come up and introduce themselves as huge fans of my writing—while a photographer walked around the restaurant, capturing internet peers becoming real-life friends.

That night was the moment I realized I was no longer an "aspiring writer."

I was a writer.

And this was only the beginning.

A few months later, I was pacing around the office talking on the phone to an editor from *Inc Magazine*.

Thanks to that event, and getting to meet Quora's team in person, I was ultimately offered the opportunity to contribute to *Inc Magazine* directly.

Everyone else at the office had gone home for the day. It was just me in my mentor's office. Staring out the window, I knew something big was happening. This was it. My writing career was about to take off.

"We expect our paid columnists to write at least four articles per month," the editor said.

Feeling like I'd been playing in the minor leagues and was being offered a contract to play in the NHL, I said, "Can I write thirty?"

Silence.

"If you think you can write thirty quality articles per month, go ahead," he said, assuming there was no way I'd be able to maintain that kind of output. *Inc Magazine* wasn't paying me per article, they were paying me per page view. In their mind, the more content, the better. In my mind, this improved my chances for success.

Now, most people in my position would have stopped writing on Quora, graduating to writing for a major publication. I didn't. I had built a massive following on Quora, and was averaging more than 1.5 million organic views per month, every month, while still having at least one of my answers republished by a major publication every single week. I was on fire, and wasn't about to throw all my hard work to the wayside.

Instead, I doubled-down on my daily writing habit, and committed to writing one answer on Quora, and one article for *Inc Magazine*, every single day.

My first month writing for *Inc Magazine*, I wrote 30 articles, and accumulated more than 300,000 page views.

They sent me a check for $3,000.

The second month, I wrote another 30 articles, and brought in more than half a million page views. I made $5,000.

For six months straight, January to June of 2016, I kept up this writing routine—while still working nine hours per day as a copywriter, while commuting an hour on the train to and from work, and while eating five meals per day and hitting the gym for an hour and a half every night. I worked. I lifted. And I wrote. And then every night when I got home from the gym around 9:00 p.m., I'd make myself a plate of gluten-free pasta, asparagus, and chicken, and work on my first memoir, *Confessions of a Teenage Gamer*, until midnight.

Until that July, four months later, I decided to quit my job.

I had already written more than 100 articles for *Inc Magazine* exclusively, and became one of their Top 10 most-read columnists. I was consistently averaging 300,000 views every month on my column, and had proven to myself that I could generate almost all of my full-time income just from writing online. I figured if I had eight more hours in the day, I could easily make up the rest being a freelancer writer.

I had dedicated four years of my life to learning the ins and outs of marketing, advertising, and copywriting.

I had learned a tremendous amount about the business of creativity from my mentor.

And I had built myself into one of the most-read writers on the internet—averaging more views, shares, and comments per month than most best-selling authors trying to do the same.

Finally, I felt ready to take the leap.

The same day I left the agency, I also published my first book.

With no marketing budget, no publishing house, no PR agency, or anything except my Quora audience and my *Inc Magazine* column, my first memoir, *Confessions of a Teenage Gamer,* reached #2 in two separate categories on Amazon in the first 24 hours. I had invested $1,000 of my own money into self-publishing a professional-looking product, and sold enough copies the first week to recoup my investment and start turning a profit.

But it wasn't until I started writing about how I was a free agent and available as a freelance writer, that I realized the game had changed.

I'd "beaten the game" of online writing.

Now, I needed to figure out how I was going to turn all that attention into a full-time income.

It was humbling for me to have spent four years on a book, only to release it into the world and sell a couple hundred copies (I couldn't exactly "live" off $82.76 per month in royalties). I wasn't discouraged, and my dream was still to become a successful author, but I needed to be realistic with myself: if I wanted to live in an apartment with a dishwasher and a shower that didn't scream at you first thing in the morning; if I wanted to not be so dependent on needing to write a viral *Inc* column every month to pay my bills; if I wanted to make more money, so I could have more time to invest in my own writing, my own books, then I needed to find something else in the meantime.

I needed to play a more profitable game.

On accident, I discovered the world of executive ghostwriting.

A former CEO who had been following me for a long time on Quora sent me an email. He'd exited his company a few years prior and was coming out with a business book—and wanted to know if I'd be willing to help him build an audience for his business writing online. Nothing super academic, nothing overly complicated. In fact, one of the things he enjoyed most about my own writing was how conversational it felt. "That style, that's what I'm looking for," he said.

One client led to two. Two led to four.

And by the end of 2016, my signature "conversational style" of writing had become the voice of more than 15 different founders, executives, and investors—quadrupling my income.

I was now a six-figure writer.

Earning real money as a writer only motivated me to work harder, and set bigger and bigger goals.

One morning, I was eating breakfast at the small table between my refrigerator and my bed. Above my head was a rotted bubble in the ceiling that looked like it was about to explode with old toilet water. My lease wasn't up for another few months.

Picking at my bowl of oatmeal, I looked out of my dirty apartment window at the tree outside. It had been months since I'd worked on any of my own writing. And even though I still wanted to write my own books, it was hard to ignore the opportunity in front of me: in a matter of months, I'd gone from making $0 as a writer to making $3,000 per month writing for *Inc Magazine* to making $20,000 per month ghostwriting opinion articles for executives. Furthermore, I'd clearly stumbled onto an opportunity very few other writers seemed to know about. I'd heard the term "ghostwriting" before, but it wasn't until my own clients started calling me their "personal ghostwriter" that I started to realize the true value of my skill set.

They weren't just hiring some freelancer.

They were hiring a dedicated specialist who could speak their language, translate their thoughts, and communicate the stories and insights they were trying to share in an organized, articulate way.

Inspired to take advantage of the opportunity I saw, I flew to Atlanta to visit one of my best friends from college—trying to convince him to quit his job and build a ghostwriting agency with me.

In his much nicer apartment, I sat at his kitchen counter with my laptop open and explained how I was ghostwriting for executives. "This is a real pain point for these people," I said. "They have so much insight to share, they're exactly who everyone would want to learn from on Quora, and they're honestly the people who deserve columns at major publications. They just don't have the time to sit down and write—or, they aren't writers, and don't want to invest in that skill set."

Drew sat there listening, trying to figure out whether I was manically trying to convince him to pursue another one of my ideas (as I'd done many times in the past), or if I was actually onto something. While we'd been long-time collaborators, I'd always been the optimist, and he was the pessimist.

"How much money are you getting paid per article though," he asked. "Fifty bucks?"

His guess made me realize how little he, and the rest of the world, understood about the business of writing online.

"Five hundred," I said. "And that's average. I've gotten as high as $1,000 per article."

"What."

"Yup."

Drew sat there letting the information sink into his brain. He'd been complaining to me for months about how unhappy he was in his job—which killed me because he was one of the most naturally entrepreneurial people I'd ever met in my life, with skill sets very different from my own. He was better with numbers, he'd been working in sales (selling fractional ownership in private jets to high net worth individuals), and was an incredible designer with a natural eye.

Together, we'd be able to build a real brand.

"Alright, I'm in," he said.

We stayed up until three in the morning that night, strategizing the company.

We called it Digital Press.

30 days later, we crossed six figures in annual recurring revenue.

At ten months, we crossed seven figures.

And by the 18-month marker, we had 20 full-time employees—editors, writers, and a sales team—and had built a multi-million-dollar business, eventually working with more than 300 different founders, C-level executives, venture capitalists, angel investors, NYT best-selling authors, Grammy-winning musicians, Olympic and professional athletes, international speakers, and more, helping them share their insights and personal stories using the same recipe I'd used to become the #1 most-read writer on all of Quora.

And now, I want to share that recipe with you.

Who is this book for?

There are a wide variety of reasons why someone would want to start writing online today.

Maybe you're an author and want to build a loyal audience of people who will consistently buy your books.

Maybe you're a freelancer and want clients and customers to see you as a professional in your field.

Maybe you're a speaker and want to use writing as another mechanism for sharing your insights and perspectives.

Maybe you're an entrepreneur and want to build credibility for yourself as a thought leader in your industry.

Maybe you're an executive and understand the value of publicly representing your company, its mission, and your point of view of the future.

Maybe you're an investor and want to share your knowledge and expertise to attract the right type of startup founders looking for funding.

Maybe you're a consultant and want decision makers to see the way you think and hire you to help their company.

The list goes on and on.

**By writing online, you elevate yourself.
And when you elevate yourself, you open
new doors of opportunity.**

It took me a long time to realize that writing online isn't
just for writers.

It's for everyone, in every industry, at every level—no
matter who you are, what you've accomplished, or where
you ultimately want to end up. By investing in yourself,
and using writing to share your insights, perspectives, and
stories with the world, you will end up accelerating your
professional career (and personal growth) in ways you
couldn't have achieved elsewhere. And by mastering "the
game" of online writing, you will ultimately reach more
people, expand your network, and become an influential
voice and leader in your industry.

I'm going to show you how to play the game, so you can:

- Accumulate thousands, tens of thousands,
  even millions of views on your writing.

- Build an audience of loyal, engaged readers,
  subscribers, followers, and customers.

- Earn badges of credibility, in the form of
  social media metrics, press acknowledgment,
  and so on.

- Connect with influential people and industry
  peers.

- Speak at major events, with masterminds,
  and on noteworthy podcasts.

- Write for major publications such as *TIME, Forbes, Fortune, Harvard Business Review, Inc Magazine, CNBC,* and dozens more.

- And turn the attention you attract (and actively maintain) on the internet into other much larger opportunities, such as landing a book deal, a high-ticket consulting project, an investor for your company, etc.

The reason I know these outcomes are possible is because I have personally experienced all of them—and so have the 300+ clients we've worked with through Digital Press, in addition to the hundreds of writers I've personally mentored over the years.

So, how do you do it?

And more importantly, where do you start?

Chapter 1

Want To Start Writing Online? Don't Start A Blog

The first thing I'm going to tell you about the art of online writing goes against conventional wisdom.

It's the first step everyone thinks to take—and it ends up being their biggest mistake.

Whenever someone tells me they want to start writing online, their first assumption is they should start a blog. When they use this word, *blog*, a very particular image comes to mind: their own website, with their own look and feel, presenting their own thoughts, linearly, post by post. The way most people imagine writing online is still rooted in 1995. They think the best path forward is to begin a "web log."

The truth is, blogging, having your own website, and writing online are three completely different things. You can blog without having your own website. You can have your own website without ever blogging. And you can write things online that millions upon millions of people read without having your own website or your own blog.

So, let's start by defining what those three words really mean.

1. The definition of a blog.

For the past 30 years, a blog was seen as a public diary. Sites like LiveJournal and Blogger were where people would publish and sequentially document their thoughts, rants, musings, and more.

Today, starting a blog is a lot closer to starting a business.

The entire purpose of starting a blog, and having people come to your own site, is for two reasons and two reasons only—and both are inspired by money. First, you either plan on monetizing your website via ads (which is why it's so crucial that people read your material on your site, *which you own*), or second, you plan on using your blog to attract a certain type of customer to your website in order to capture their email address and/or sell them a product, service, etc.

Now, most people hear the above and think, "Well, of course my goal is to make money from my writing." But making money from your writing is not the same thing as 1) starting a website monetized through ads (which is a media business) or 2) starting a website that sells a product or service (which could be anything from a physical product to an information product like an online course), which are all different variations of an e-commerce business.

Either way, when you start a "blog," you aren't really in the business of writing.

You're in the business of ads, products, or services.

2. The definition of a website.

For the vast majority of people, the primary purpose of having a website is to quickly communicate who you are, what you do, and what you have done in the past.

In short, it's a business card.

A perfect example would be the personal website of an author and speaker. Let's say someone says, "Hey, you absolutely have to check out Nicolas Cole's work. He's incredible." If you have no idea who I am, the first thing you're going to do is Google my name. Of all the links that appear on the first page, you are most likely going to click on my website first (since someone's personal website is usually the link that ranks the highest). Once you're on my website, you are going to go through a series of judgments in your mind: "What does Cole do? Do I see any symbols of credibility? Do I recognize any of his work, or anyone he has worked with? Does this look like someone worth knowing about?"

Once these judgments have been made, and if you're still curious to learn more, you're going to then navigate deeper in order to find some of my writing. If I have a blog on my website, you might start there—and if I don't have a blog, that doesn't mean you're just going to stop looking. Instead, you're going to go back to your Google search and start clicking on other links in order to find what you're looking for: my Quora profile, my Medium, LinkedIn, or Instagram profiles, my Amazon Author page, etc. In fact, even if I *do* have a blog, you're probably still going to go through this research process—because what you're really interested in is seeing my writing *in the context of how other people feel about my writing too.*

Which is why, unless you are an internet entrepreneur looking to build a media business (monetize through ads) or focus 100% of your efforts on selling a product (monetize through e-commerce), I wholeheartedly believe starting a blog is a waste of time.

And to be perfectly honest, even if you are selling a product (as I eventually did), there are far more effective ways to get exposure, build a brand, and bring traffic to your personal website than "blogging."

3. The definition of Online Writing.

The way I define Online Writing is based on one variable and one variable only:

Sharing **thoughts, stories, opinions, and insights** *on a platform that already has an active audience.*

If you're writing funny restaurant reviews on Yelp where there are millions and millions of users, I would put that in the bucket of Online Writing. If you are an opinion columnist at a digital publication that gets tens of millions of page views each month, I'd call that Online Writing. If you regularly share industry insights in the form of quick status updates on LinkedIn, Twitter, or Facebook, that's Online Writing. I would even argue that if you are contributing a guest post to *someone else's* website or blog, where they already have an engaged audience, that's Online Writing.

- If you are writing on your own platform hoping an audience will come to you, that's Blogging.

- And if you are bringing your voice to

a platform where an audience already exists, that's Online Writing.

The reason I am so wholeheartedly against blogging as a writing strategy is because starting a blog means starting a new website, and starting a new website means starting with zero traffic.

And how do you get traffic to your blog?

A) Spend money on ads (direct people from other websites over to your website).

B) Optimize your blog posts for Search Engine Optimization (SEO) so they'll appear on the first page of Google when people search certain keywords and phrases.

C) Build a social media following on another platform (Facebook, Twitter, Instagram, etc.) and direct people to your website via links.

But here's the thing: none of the above have anything to do with sharing your *thoughts, stories, opinions, and insights* at scale. Ads, SEO, and social media marketing are very different skills than the art of writing and the science of attracting organic attention.

Writers don't typically have an advertising budget (I certainly didn't)—and the ones who do, want to spend it on something with a more concrete return on investment (like selling a product or service). Writers also don't want to spend time trying to figure out how to "growth hack" a social media following on another platform just so they can funnel people to their blog. Most of all, writers don't want to stuff their blog posts full of keywords in the name of ranking better on Google.

What writers and industry leaders want is to share their knowledge in the right ways, on the right platforms, and have people hear what they have to say.

What they want is to *write*.

So, when should you start a blog?

There are two scenarios where starting with a blog is actually the right decision.

The first scenario is if you are a business selling some sort of product or service, and revenue is the primary outcome you are looking to drive.

Not credibility.

Not exposure.

Not building an audience.

Not industry perception or social reach.

Revenue **tied to a specific product or service.**

Hubspot, for example, is a company that sells CRM software. Their blog isn't really much of a blog at all. It operates much closer to an industry publication for digital marketers, and their strategy is to publish so much high-quality content that if you are searching for anything marketing related on Google, you'll end up on their website, discover their CRM tool, and become a customer. In order to do this effectively, Hubspot employs and curates work from hundreds upon hundreds of contributing writers, creating a content marketing machine.

If you are a company with a product or service to sell, and you have the means to create a "digital media company" within your niche, HubSpot is a terrific use case for having an active blog on your website. Your blog should become an industry publication, where the purpose of that publication is to tap into search traffic around specific keywords and increase the likelihood of a reader becoming a customer looking to buy your product or service.

The second scenario for starting a blog is the solopreneur, the digital marketer, the fitness coach, the individual who is less concerned with sharing his or her own individual insights and perspectives, and instead wants to use writing as a marketing mechanism for their internet business. These types of websites aren't really about the individual as much as they are the topic (and product) they are looking to sell. Sure, some of the best travel or nutrition or fitness bloggers end up sharing a good amount about their own lives in the process, but their blog content is primarily focused on providing informative answers to popular questions *directly related to their product or service.*

One of the best examples I've ever seen is a website called Kindlepreneur. This is an entire website dedicated to educating self-published authors on how to optimize and maximize their self-publishing efforts. It's an absolute behemoth of a website, insanely informative, and constructed in a way where if you are the target audience, you can't help but find your way to the site, devour the free blog content, type your email into one of the many opt-in forms for more detailed information, and even purchase one of the products (I did).

The important thing I'd like to point out, however, is that when I thought to include this example, the writer's name wasn't what came to mind. What came to mind was Kindlepreneur, the name of the site—and if you go to the site yourself, you'll see that's the way it's presented on the front page. *Kindlepreneur with Dave Chesson.*

In this sense, Dave's blog has almost nothing to do with sharing and scaling *his own thoughts, stories, opinions, and insights*, and is more centered around building a brand and "ultimate encyclopedia" of knowledge for anything related to one singular topic: self-publishing.

> If you are a company with the resources to build and scale your website into an industry publication, you should start a blog. And if you are a solopreneur who wants to "own" a category or niche by creating a directory of knowledge, you should start a blog. **But if you don't fit within either of these two categories, then blogging is not your best path forward.**

Now, there is a third scenario where you can be a successful "blogger." However, it is an outlier scenario, and not one I would recommend. Maybe five or ten years ago. But not anymore.

The example that comes to mind here is Mark Manson.

For those who can't place the name, Mark Manson is the author of the bright orange book that took over every bookstore from 2017 to 2020, *The Subtle Art Of Not Giving A F*ck.*

Most people don't know that Manson started blogging on his own website, www.markmanson.net, more than a decade ago (hence why I believe this strategy is outdated, but I digress). Slowly but surely, he gained a following for his musings related to personal development, and even says overtly on his About page, "Most of what I write is written for myself, first and foremost."

This is the purest form of blogging.

When Manson crossed over into the world of Online Writing was the moment he started using data to inform decisions that brought him outside of his personal website. As the story goes, *The Subtle Art Of Not Giving A F*ck* was actually one of Manson's most popular blog posts, which was then expanded on and turned into a book (the logic being: "If millions of people resonate with a blog post on this topic, surely they would enjoy a longer version."). *The Subtle Art* went on to become a #1 *New York Times* best seller with more than six million copies sold.

The reason I say Manson's approach is outdated is because newer, better tools have been created in the past ten years that make the process of building your name, audience, and credibility as a writer exponentially faster.

When Manson first started his website and blog, websites like Medium and Quora didn't exist. You couldn't publish articles yet on LinkedIn. Blogger was still one of the best publishing platforms on the internet (and to be honest, it wasn't that good). Facebook and Twitter were infants. YouTube was just starting to turn "vloggers" into internet celebrities. And the term "influencer" didn't even exist yet. Every benefit that came with having a blog a decade ago can now be achieved in 1/100th the amount of time—if you understand how to play the game of capturing and keeping people's attention online.

"But Cole, you were selling eBooks on your website. Why didn't you start blogging to drive sales?"

Great question.

In 2015, after I wrote my first massively viral article on Quora and self-published my first two eBooks, I now had a product to sell.

The reason I chose not to pivot from Quora and start writing on my personal website was because I wasn't passionate about building an encyclopedia site for fitness readers. My near-term goal might have been to drive eBook sales for my "Skinny to Shredded" series, but my long-term goal wasn't to build a revenue-generating website selling fitness eBooks, fitness programs, and online fitness courses. If that had been my goal, then like the Kindlepreneur example, I would have launched something like www.skinnytoshredded.com, writing hyper-focused content about fitness, and specifically targeting keywords and phrases potential customers were searching on Google.

Again, the difference here comes down to what you want to get out of your writing. Do you want to build a company and brand, making money selling ads, products, and/or services? Then a website and "blog" makes sense. But if you enjoy writing and want to build a personal brand, position yourself as an authentic voice in your industry, and share your *thoughts, stories, opinions, and insights at scale,* then do not start a blog.

The Online Writing approach was made for you.

Chapter **2**

The New Way To Think About Being A Writer In The Digital Age

Data.

Data is the single greatest indicator of what's working (and what isn't working) about your writing.

We take for granted the fact that writers haven't always had access to readily available feedback. If you were an author in the late 1900s, you had to share excerpts of your novel-in-progress at grungy bars and restaurants hoping someone would enlighten you with how they felt about your writing. If you were a newspaper columnist in the 1970s and 80s, you were a bit more fortunate, learning whether the masses enjoyed your column the following month or week it was published. But it wasn't until the late 90s and early 2000s that "the feedback loop" started to shrink from months and weeks to days, hours, minutes, and eventually, seconds.

> **There are 2 types of writers today:** those who use data to inform and improve their writing, and those who fail.

When I was younger, I thought in order to be a true writer I needed to go about things a certain way.

I thought I needed to be like the old-school writers who slaved away on their manuscripts for years before unveiling their work to the world. I thought I needed to go through the more formal process of submitting my work to a publishing house and then waiting for them to give me the approval, *the permission*, to become a "professional writer." I thought I needed to walk the path of a conventional author in order to be successful.

But by the time I graduated college with a degree in fiction writing, I had a really hard time believing this tried-and-true path was still the best path forward. In fact, in my last class of the semester my senior year, our teacher said he was going to explain how we could go about "getting published." Eagerly, we all pulled out our notepads and pens and looked at him, ready to hear the secret process for becoming a "professional writer."

"The first thing you're going to want to do," he said, "is print off a copy of your manuscript." I wrote that down.

"Next, you're going to want to do some research on the publishing houses who have published other authors writing similar things to you, and keep their names and addresses somewhere handy." I wrote that down too.

"Finally, you're going to want to place copies of your manuscript into manila envelopes, mail them to each publishing house on your list, and then wait."

I didn't write that step down. I raised my hand instead.

"For how long?" I said, not bothering to wait for him to call on me.

My teacher—a shy, quirky playwright and fiction novelist—did not like me very much.

"You wait until you hear a response," he said, frustrated I'd just interrupted him.

"And how long is that?" I asked again. The look on every other student's face was pure fear. They wanted to know how long they were going to have to wait too.

"Sometimes it can take up to six months for them to respond," he said, in that tone parents use when they're trying to tell you things were hard for them and so they should be hard for you too.

"SIX MONTHS?" I said. "That makes no sense."

The rest of the class clearly agreed, nodding with me.

"Well that's the way it is," he said, and proceeded to move on with the lesson.

After I'd graduated, I started researching other ways to build myself as a writer on the internet.

And most of what I found was disappointing.

All the advice I read was retroactive. The most popular publishing strategy was to finish my book or product, and then as I was "preparing to launch," go ballistic with press and ads and blog posts—all of which required a huge investment of either time or money or both.

In my mind, this approach seemed backward: why would a writer wait until the moment they were ready to publish their product to start building their audience? The more logical path forward would be to start writing online, build an audience, learn what people actually wanted from you, and THEN launch your product.

So that's what I did.

The new way to think about being a writer in the digital age is to turn your writing into a data mining machine.

Today, the vast majority of the advising work I do with writers, authors, industry leaders, and companies, is to get them to flip this script.

99% of people *think they know* what they should write about.

They *think* they know who their audience is. They *think* they know what book they should write. They *think* they know which part of their story is going to resonate with the most people. They *think* they know "who they are"—and the brutal truth is, they don't. They have assumptions. They have educated guesses. But they have zero data that can confirm whether or not they're correct. And of course, the second mistake they make (after selling their book proposal to a big fancy publisher, or retaining a PR firm to "amplify their digital presence") is they think to themselves, "It's time I have my own website. I need to start a blog."

This is why I tell everyone—whether you're an aspiring author or the CEO of a public company—that before you do anything, before you write your book, before you launch your product, before you think about "positioning yourself," you need to write online.

Why?

- **Writing online, first, reduces your risk:** You will learn what people like and don't like much faster, for free.

- **Writing online, first, helps you find your voice:** If you start paying attention to data, the way you write today will not be the way you write tomorrow.

- **Writing online, first, builds your audience from day one:** Instead of waiting until your bigger projects are ready to be shared, you will set yourself up for success from the very beginning.

- **Writing online, first, will give you insight into what people want:** This is what Mark Manson did that was so brilliant. He used the data from his blog to inform the title, structure, and concept for his book, *The Subtle Art of Not Giving A F*ck*.

As soon as I started writing every day on Quora, I started to realize how much faster I was learning, growing, and publishing on the internet. Anytime I would write something online, I would receive immediate feedback—in the form of words ("I totally agree! Amazing perspective," or, "You're an idiot. Go die in a fire,") and in the form of data (Views, Likes, Shares, Upvotes, Comments, etc.).

Without even realizing it, I would then take that data and use it to inform my next piece of writing. I would double-down on topics that attracted more viewership. I would retell stories that had prompted people to Comment. I would adjust my headlines and the format of my articles based on previous articles that had performed best.

All of a sudden, I was no longer making decisions based on what I thought people wanted.

People told me what they wanted—all I had to do was listen.

This is your "Writing Data Flywheel."

Your "Writing Data Flywheel" is a mechanism for endless inspiration.

The sooner you start receiving feedback on your writing, the faster you will grow as a writer. The more data you can gather, the more insight you'll have into what people want; the more your writing will resonate; the more people you will reach, and so on.

Likes = "This is something I approve of. Nice job."

Shares = "This is something more people need to know about. This represents me."

Comments = "This is thought provoking. I agree/disagree, and I want you to know why.

Views = "This strikes a chord. There's something valuable here."

Now, why don't people like this approach? Why do so many

people insist on pursuing the path to becoming a writer the old way?

The answer is because they're *afraid*.

Writing online, and the immediacy of the feedback, prompts a high amount of anxiety. It's the same reason people are afraid to speak in front of a crowd—the feedback is immediate (you can see how people feel by the looks on their faces). But it's this back-and-forth, this instant reveal that also makes the process so valuable. The faster you can gather feedback in the form of data, the faster you can make decisions to move yourself forward. Conversely, the more you delay this feedback, the longer it's going to take you to figure out "what's working" and what's not.

Which is why I believe it is so important to Practice In Public.

Practicing in public is how you gather that data in the first place.

My entire life, I've been fascinated by musicians and performers who rose to mega-stardom. And if you look closely, you'll find nearly all of them share something in common.

Justin Bieber was playing the guitar on the sidewalk singing full volume before he was even a teenager.

Ed Sheeran played in subways for years before being signed by a record label.

The Beatles played together six nights a week at a strip club in Hamburg, Germany, before becoming mega famous.

Taylor Swift played at Rotary Clubs and county fairs all over Nashville before becoming one of the biggest artists in the world.

Eminem, 2pac, Notorious B.I.G, and every rapper before the digital age started by rapping in their local communities, on street corners and at house parties, before taking over the radio waves.

The list goes on and on.

What introduced me to this idea of "practicing in public" was really my family. I grew up in a household where there was always a musical instrument being played. Either my sister was practicing the violin, or my younger brother was practicing the piano, or my youngest brother was practicing the violin, or the piano, or the guitar. We were all required to play a musical instrument and to be classically trained.

But every time I would sit down to practice the piano, I knew that if I repeatedly played the wrong note or chord, my mother would shout from the other side of the house, "It's C sharp! Not D sharp!" I'd then look down at my hands and whisper, "You think I don't know that, Mom." It was one of the most frustrating parts of having a constant audience—and at the same time, it made me a talented pianist. In elementary school, I was playing Beethoven, Mozart, and Bach. By middle school, I had graduated to Haydn and Liszt. And by high school, I could play entire sonatas with my eyes closed. There was something about knowing she, and the other members of my family, were always listening that made me care more about the way I played the piano.

I noticed this same growth process happen when I started my gaming blog as a teenager.

I will never forget, in one of my first blog posts on the internet, I had used the wrong "their" throughout the entire blog. I should have written "they're." When I woke up the next morning, someone had commented, "You must be a teenager because your sense of grammar is nauseating. Learn the difference between their and they're you idiot. You should just stop blogging and go kill yourself."

When I read that comment—well first of all, everybody told everybody to kill themselves in the gaming world so that wasn't anything out of the ordinary. But when I read that comment, I felt really insecure about my writing. This person had pointed out a mistake I'd made and shamed me for it. But the thought of quitting and never writing anything ever again seemed even more ridiculous. All I needed to do was Google the difference between the two words and not make the same mistake again.

That piece of feedback was harsh. But it was also the moment I learned the difference between "their" and "they're"—and I remembered it for the rest of my life.

Practicing In Public is what separates aspiring writers from professional writers.

In life, a lot of people *talk* about doing the thing they want to do. They talk and they imagine and they brainstorm and they keep their work hidden and all the while, they convince themselves what they're doing is brilliant. They are waiting, waiting for the perfect moment to reveal their amazing work to the world—and then, *then*, everyone will see.

But very few ever exit the "waiting" stage.

And then there are those who don't hide. They don't wait. They start and they play their guitar right there on the sidewalk and they pay close attention to who smiles and who doesn't, which songs people stop to listen to and which ones they ignore. They play and they play and they play so much they could play anytime—they don't need to wait for "the perfect opportunity," or for the lights, the stage, or the setting to be just right. They know how to do what they do best, simply because they've done it so much in public—and stage or no stage, lights or no lights, won't make a difference.

People who don't Practice In Public are trying to mitigate their risk.

They want the publishing deal to tell them "they're a professional writer" before they put themselves out there to be judged. They want the press to say, "This is the person you've all been waiting for," before they even step on stage. Deep down, they really, really don't believe in their own skills, and so they want to create the perfect scenario that tells the world, "This is someone worth listening to," because they haven't actually gone through the hard work of figuring that out for themselves yet. They don't know if they're someone worth listening to—because they haven't put their skills to the test.

I believe the only way to overcome this fear is to run directly at it.

And it's in running directly at it that you become the person "worth listening to" in the first place.

Chapter 3

How The Online Writing Game Works: 7 Levels Of Success

Writing online is a competition, plain and simple.

We can call it art—and it is. We can call it a business—and it's that too. But at the end of the day, the reason a reader reads one piece of writing and doesn't read another is because somewhere in their mind, they are making a choice. And in that choice is a decision to pick one writer's work over another.

Which means one writer wins, and the other writer loses.

On the internet, especially, every single creator—whether you're a writer, a podcaster, a video maker, a photographer—is competing for attention. Which means, as a writer, you aren't just competing against other writers. You're also competing against cat videos and viral memes and all the other types of content someone could consume in a day.

Unfortunately, most people don't see the internet this way. Instead, their measure for success is more binary. If they write a blog post, they've succeeded. If they don't write a blog post, they've failed. If a couple people read their post, it must have been "Good." And if nobody reads their post, well, then it must have been "Bad." And because their measures for success are so black and white, they tend to spend money on all the wrong things to drive exposure, increase their audience, and build their credibility: a better-looking website, a bigger advertising budget, more PR, more promotions, *more, more, more.*

But the truth is, the real reason most people aren't successful writing online has very little to do with all the bells and whistles that surround the writing.

Their biggest problem is the writing itself.

They don't understand how the game works.

Level 1: Conscious vs Unconscious

My personal belief is that every single person on the internet, whether they realize it or not, is playing "the game."

The game is simple. When you post a piece of content—whether it's a picture of you and your family on Facebook, or a video of you jumping into a pool in a bikini on Instagram, or a link to a *New York Times* article on LinkedIn—you are sharing a part of yourself *at scale.* The more you share, the more people learn about you. The more people learn about you, the more conversations happen, the more opportunities present themselves, and the more a scalable digital version of your real-life self begins to crystalize on the internet.

Now, some people like to believe they are not playing "the game." The way they rationalize this is by saying, "I don't really care what people think of what I post. I just share things I care about." What they fail to realize, however, is that posting a picture of them and their grandma, and an Instagram model posing in front of a lime green

Lamborghini, are the exact same "thing." They are both representations of the creator's self, expressed digitally. The only difference is: one person is playing the game consciously, and the other is playing the game unconsciously.

Another way of saying this would be "intentionally" vs "unintentionally."

I'd like to clarify what I'm saying here by reiterating: I do not think every single person on earth *should* strive to be a "social media influencer." I would just like to point out that whether we like it or not, we are all playing "the game" as long as we're on the internet. Which means, Level 1 is all about answering the question, "Am I playing this game consciously? Am I achieving my goal? Or am I playing this game unconsciously, and do I not care where I end up?"

Successful writers play the game of Online Writing consciously. Unsuccessful writers play the game unconsciously—and then wonder why they aren't succeeding.

If you truly have no desire to be a professional writer, and exclusively see the craft as your own personal hobby, then please, feel free to write whatever it is you want to write about. Post it wherever your heart desires (your blog, for example). After all, life isn't all about "winning"—the purpose of life is to play, learn, explore, and express. So again, if all you want is your art in your own corner of the web, by all means, throw this book in the trash and live your best life.

But here's the thing. If you say that's what writing means to you, and only two people clap for what you wrote, then you aren't allowed to complain. You can't sit there and blame the internet or "the algorithm" or all the people on planet earth who "don't know great writing." You have to accept the fact that you've chosen to play the game unconsciously (that is to say, *without any awareness or desire to pay attention to how readers react and respond to your work*), which means you're stuck in the two-clap club.

However, if your goal is to be better tomorrow than you are today, you have to play the game consciously.

You have to start opening your eyes to the way the game is played, who your competition is, and what they're doing that is capturing (and keeping) people's attention—so that you can do the same.

I'm not asking you to compromise your authentic writing voice for clickbait trash.

I'm telling you that by playing the game with intention, and paying attention to the data, you will discover and amplify your most authentic writing voice ten times faster.

Level 2: Choose A Category

Most people have no idea what category they're actually writing in.

For example, when you write about yoga, are you in the yoga category? Or are you in the comedy category since what you're writing about are funny experiences showing up to yoga classes? When you write about technology, are you in the technology-tutorial category, because you're teaching people how to use a certain piece of technology? Or are you in the technology-news category, because you're writing about the impact this technology is going to have on the industry?

The entire—and I mean this quite literally, the ENTIRE—art and business and "game" of online writing is rooted in understanding what category you're actually competing within. Unless you can consciously name the category, you will never have a firm grasp as to whether your work is "Better" or "Worse" than the competition. It isn't until you understand the category, and see "The Ladder" that exists within your category, that you can begin climbing your way to the top.

There is another strategy here, and that's to not compete within an existing category but create an entirely new category of your own. However, before we get into breaking the rules, it's important to learn the rules of the game, first.

What is a category?

A category is a frame, a bucket, a spot on the shelf where similar objects reside. Imagine you walk into a bookstore. Where do you go? Most people aren't aware of it, but the very first thought they have when they walk into a bookstore is, "What category am I looking for?" If they're looking for a thriller set in a courtroom, they're going to go to the fiction -> thriller -> law category. If they're looking for a business book about positive workplace habits they're going to go to the nonfiction -> business -> productivity category. And so on.

It isn't until the individual is within a category that they ask themselves, "Who is the single best writer in this category? Who should I read?" If they went to the fiction -> thriller -> law category, they would undoubtedly discover John Grisham. If they already knew and loved John Grisham, then they would stop their search there. And if they didn't like John Grisham, or if they were new to the category altogether, they would then start comparing John Grisham to David Baldacci, Scott Turow, and so on.

Categories are how we organize information in our minds. Know your category and you'll know **where readers 'fit' you into their own minds.**

Categories are also how we decide what it is we want to buy—or at the very least, give our attention.

The exact same mental process happens on the internet. In fact, every website and social media algorithm is organized by category. Go to any publication and you'll find thousands upon thousands of articles organized by category: technology, lifestyle, food, sports, news, politics, business, and so on. On static websites and blogs, these categories are created manually by the owner of the site. And on social media sites, these categories are created intuitively— the more you scroll, the more your algorithm knows what "categories" you like, and so on.

This is what makes writing online a strategy game.

Think of every category as its own playing field with its own rules. What's considered kosher in one category may seem completely unconventional in another. What one category calls "innovative," another might see as boring. Your job is to take the time to read, observe, and study your chosen category to the point where you understand its native language. You should be able to hear the nuances in how people communicate, know which formats have become tried and true, and most importantly, name the dominant writers within the category you are aiming to surpass.

Level 3: Define Your "Style" (Where Do You Sit On The Writing Spectrum?)

All writing exists on a spectrum, and that spectrum looks something like this.

Educating <<<>>> Entertaining

On the left-hand side you have writing that informs and explains (textbooks, news, nonfiction, etc.) and on the right-hand side you have writing that captivates and entertains (true stories, fiction stories, etc.).

As you begin to play the game of online writing consciously, the next big question you have to ask yourself is which side of the fence are you going to play on? Are you a non-fiction writer? Or are you a fiction writer? Are you an educational writer, where your mission is to inform and explain? Or are you an entertainment writer, where your mission is to captivate and entertain?

Textbook writers, historians, and journalists exist on the far left-hand side.

Sci-fi writers, pop culture bloggers, and sitcom screenwriters exist on the far right.

And all along the middle are writers and creators who straddle the line, some educating more than entertaining, others entertaining more than educating.

Creating a unique, memorable, and "different" writing style is nothing more than a deliberate choice to sit somewhere unexpected on this Writing Spectrum. The more unexpected the style, *in the context of your category*, the more likely you are to stand out. On the other hand, the more expected the style, *in the context of your category*, the more likely you are to sound like everyone else—and blend into the noise.

If you want to know why every company in a specific industry sounds the same, it's because all their messaging is "expected." But when a new company comes along and their messaging is "unexpected," suddenly they stand out.

The secret to creating a unique writing style is by **doing what would be considered 'unexpected' in your chosen category.**

If everyone in your category is writing restaurant reviews as if they're formal essays, something "unexpected" would be to write comedic restaurant reviews from the perspective of a part-time food blogger named Cindy who works for a failing restaurant magazine, and shows up to every restaurant pretending to be this hot insta-famous food-review writer but actually doesn't know anything about food and gets too drunk at every tasting (and it shows in her writing).

In the professional-restaurant-review category, this would be "unexpected."

And as a result, it would stand out.

A clear sign you've executed this successfully is people within your chosen category (both readers and writers) will comment on the unexpectedness of your style. Some will support it, letting you know how refreshing this "new voice" is in the category. And others will feel threatened by it, pointing out how it "goes against the rules" that have been previously defined. As a result, you will experience both positive and negative engagement—again, forcing readers and other writers to make a clear choice: which side of the fence do they stand on? Do they support your style? Or are they against it?

I cannot stress enough here how impossible it is to know these things about yourself and your own writing at the very beginning. My recommendation here would not be to sit at your desk and think endlessly about what your unique style is. My recommendation would be for you to get started writing, publishing, gathering data, "practicing in public," and studying The Ladder of your chosen category. Over time, data will reveal which parts of your writing voice are resonating (and which parts are falling flat), and as long as you keep paying attention to the feedback you're receiving, your voice will continue to grow and evolve.

Chances are, where you end up won't be what you had originally thought people wanted.

And that's a good thing.

Level 4: Optimize Your Writing Style For Speed

We can debate all day long about what makes "Good" writing (remember though, "Good" is subjective and an inefficient way of measuring effectiveness), but the one thing I can tell you is the internet does not always favor what's "Good."

The internet favors what's *fast*.

When people read online, they don't actually "read." What they do is skim. Browse. Scroll. They let their eyes gloss over the words, and if something compelling catches their eye in the first two, five, maybe ten seconds (a word, a subhead, a phrase), *then* they'll stop skimming and start reading. But you better believe as soon as momentum in the writing starts to slow, they're gone. They'll swipe back to their social media feed and be neck deep in Memeville in a millisecond.

> When I was in college, one of my teachers used to say all the time, "If your story is reliant on the reader making it past the first few pages, then chances are, **your story doesn't need those pages.**"

I took that advice to heart when I started writing on Quora.

Instead of taking the time to give all this backstory, or make the reader wait and wait for me to "get to the point," I would just start with the main point instead. This became a defining characteristic of my writing style. I would give a few sentences of explanation or story, and immediately move on to the next point, and then to the next point, and so on and so forth.

My teachers in college called this, "The Rate of Revelation."

This is the rate at which you reveal new information to the reader—and new information is what keeps people interested. For example, a paragraph with a very slow Rate of Revelation would look something like this:

*I walked into the kitchen to grab a glass of water, which
I needed before I could continue writing. I stood there for
a while, staring inside the refrigerator. The kitchen floor
was cold under my bare feet, and even though I'd just eaten
dinner, I found myself eyeing the hummus on the second
shelf, wondering if I should grab the chips from on top of
the freezer and go for round two. I stood there and thought
about it some more.*

That paragraph has a slow Rate of Revelation because even
though it's descriptive, and maybe even entertaining, it
doesn't do much to advance the story forward. In a single
paragraph this might not seem like the end of the world,
but when an 800-word article on the internet has this slow
of a pace all the way through, you can bet only a handful
of people are going to have the patience to make it to the
end.

Now, here's what a paragraph with an extremely high Rate
of Revelation looks like.

*I walked into the kitchen to grab a glass of water. As soon
as I reached for the glass in the cabinet, it fell to the floor
and shattered, glass flying into my foot. I screamed, blood
squirting out of the tops of my toes. My neighbor, who could
hear me through the walls, came rushing over, knocking
furiously on my door. I yelled, "COME IN AND HELP ME!"
But when the door flung open, I turned around and my
neighbor had an axe in his hand. Before I could say another
word, the axe soared through the air toward my neck,
decapitating my head.*

What makes this paragraph "feel" faster is the fact that so
many **actions** are forcing the story forward. It takes all
of five sentences to go from an innocent glass of water to

an ill-intentioned neighbor slicing the main character's head off. That's a ton of *new* information packed into one paragraph.

But maybe you aren't a story writer. Maybe you're more of an information writer (closer to the left-hand side of the Writing Spectrum). Here's what a really slow paragraph would look like in the writing world of advice and education.

The one thing everyone should know about habits is they are difficult to build. In fact, habits can take years to develop. Why they take such a long time is because each one of us has a hard time with different aspects of our life, and so it can take months, even years, to pinpoint which of those aspects has the most "bad habits," and what we can do to make those bad habits more productive. But pinpointing the bad habits you want to change is really only the first step. It takes a long time after the fact in order to start seeing meaningful progress.

Pffft. Boringggggg.

The reason this paragraph feels so stale is because it's not actually revealing anything new to the reader. The idea that "habits are difficult to build" is literally the only point being made. You could delete every sentence except the first one and that "paragraph" wouldn't lose any of its value. If anything, it would gain value for the reader, because now you're not wasting their time.

Here's what a really fast paragraph looks like.

The one thing everyone should know about habits is they are difficult to build—for four reasons. First, finding the motivation to break bad habits is easier said than done (and are oftentimes used as coping mechanisms for deeper issues). Second, habits can take upwards of thirty days to form, and that's a long time investment for most people. Third, positive habits don't always show rewards right away, which make bad habits easier to fall back into. And fourth, habits tend to be a reflection of people's group of friends, which is a much harder variable to change overnight.

Most people aren't able to articulate why this second paragraph is more compelling to read than the first. Yes, it's more specific. Yes, it's "better written." But the real reason it "wins" is because its Rate of Revelation is so much higher. Every single sentence advances the "story" to the next main point. And on the internet, this level of velocity is crucial to hooking and keeping a reader's attention.

Again, I'd like to clarify that what I'm advocating for here isn't to "dumb your writing down." Some writing styles actually stand out because of their slow Rate of Revelation. And so the answer isn't just to go "faster." The point is to understand that the internet moves fast, and then reflect on the role "speed" can play *in your writing style,* **in the context of your chosen category.**

Level 5: Specificity Is The Secret

Once you decide to play the online writing game consciously...

Once you know what category you're competing in...

Once you see where your style sits on the Writing Spectrum...

Once you become aware of your Rate of Revelation...

The only thing left to do is be *the most specific writer in your chosen category.*

If you've ever found yourself on a company website that says, "We tell human stories," then you know exactly what I'm talking about. Big, vague, all-encompassing phrases lack any and all specificity. What people are trying to do when they speak in these overarching terms is try to "make something for everyone." As a result, they end up creating "something for no one." And because their messaging lacks specificity, everything they say sounds like white noise.

Being hyper-specific, on the other hand, forces a choice. It requires the reader to either jump up and down and shout, "HELL YES!" or immediately walk away. The title of this book is a perfect example. I could have made the title, "The Art of Writing." Instead, I made the title more specific: *The Art and Business of **Online** Writing.* Now the reader has to make a choice. Are they looking for insight into writing, in general? Or are they looking for insight *specific to the digital landscape.* Do they want a foofy motivational book about writing, in general? Or are they hungry to learn about the business side of publishing and *how to turn their words into cash?*

The inverse rule of "Specificity is the Secret," is
'The Broader You Are, The More Confusing You Are.'

Once you understand the role specificity plays in highly effective writing, you will start to see it everywhere.

- **"I want to learn how to cook" is broad.** "I want to learn how to cook Chicken Tikka Masala" is more specific.

- **"I'm looking to buy a car" is broad.** "I'm looking to buy an electric car" is more specific.

- **"I like writing about sports" is broad.** "I like writing about basketball and the qualities all great players have in common" is more specific.

- **"She walked into the store" is broad.** "She dragged her feet as she walked into the bodega" is more specific.

- **"He saved his money every day" is broad.** "He saved his money by placing a single dollar bill in a shoebox under his bed every night before bed" is more specific.

Ineffective writing is nothing more than *writing that does not resonate*. And the reason it doesn't resonate is almost always a reflection of specificity—or lack thereof. Either the writer isn't being specific enough about their category, or the content of their writing isn't speaking specifically to their target reader.

From a category perspective, there is a big difference between broad, overarching categories, and niche categories. It's one thing to say, "I write about life," and it's another to say, "I write about lifestyle habits for people in their 20s struggling to find their passion." A lot of aspiring writers shy away from naming their writing that specifically, because they fear putting themselves in a box. But especially when you're first starting out online, a box is *exactly* what you want. You *want* people to know where to put you on the bookshelf in their mind.

This is how broad categories become subcategories, or niche categories.

By "niching down," you will eventually uncover one small piece of the overarching category to call your own. For example, one of the overarching categories I write about often is Marketing. But there are a lot of different forms of marketing: content marketing, guerilla marketing, Google Adwords, Facebook Ads, the list goes on and on. So which niche category am I actually competing in? Which "Ladder" am I going to try to climb? Instead of trying to be "something for everyone" by writing broadly about all of these categories at once, I am better off "niching down" until I find one (or a few) categories I can dominate.

For example:

- **"Marketing" is broad.** "Content Marketing" is more specific.

- **"Content Marketing" is still too broad.** "Content Marketing For High-Growth Businesses" is more specific.

- **"Content Marketing For High-Growth Businesses" is still too broad.** "Content Marketing For Founders And Executives Of High-Growth Businesses" is more specific.

Notice, the more specific I get, the more I am forcing potential readers to make a choice. Either this is going to be *exactly what they're looking for,* or they're going to know right away I'm not the right writer for them. In addition, the more specific I am, the more I as a writer also gain clarity around what it is **I'm actually writing about—** which, in turn, makes the reader feel like they've found the exact writer they've been looking for.

As you continue to refine which specific category you're writing in (and this is an ongoing process), you then have the opportunity to bring that same specificity into the writing itself.

- **"Marketing is a great way to build exposure," is a broad statement.** "Content marketing is a great way to build exposure for your business" is more specific.

- **"Content marketing is a great way to build exposure for your business," is still a broad statement.** "Content marketing is a great way to introduce new customers to your business and move them to the top of your sales funnel" is more specific.

- **"Content marketing is a great way to introduce new customers to your business and move them to the top of your sales funnel," is still a broad statement.** "Content marketing, when published by your executive team opposed to your company's blog, is a highly effective way to build organic exposure and trust with your target customers, moving them through your sales funnel without them feeling 'sold to,'" is more specific.

It's this level of attention to detail that makes one writer "Better" than another. This is what I mean when I say "Good" and "Bad" are unproductive ways of looking at writing. The real question you should never stop asking yourself is, "Could this be more specific?" Because the more specific you can be, the more likely you are to *resonate with your target reader MORE than your competition.*

Start within a niche, and then expand from there.

Level 6: Engineering Credibility

Credibility is not the key to becoming a popular writer.

If you notice, Levels 1 through 5 have absolutely nothing to do with credibility, perception, status, brand, name recognition, PR, advertising budget, and so on. They have to do with learning the rules of the game and mastering the art of online writing.

Unfortunately, a lot of people don't want to take the time to learn the game. They'd much rather get to the part where people know who they are and start giving them external approval. Especially if the individual has already achieved some level of professional success elsewhere, they expect the very first thing they write online to be a massive success. They believe their professional status should be enough for people to pay attention to their writing.

When I first started writing on Quora, I had zero credibility.

I was a 23 year old with long hair down that curled past my ears and practically touched my shoulders. I had a degree in fiction writing, no portfolio, and my full-time job was to write social media copy. I was far from someone "successful" ready to grace the internet with expertise and wisdom.

In order for me to "win" at the game of online writing, I didn't have the luxury of leaning on my previous successes or professional titles to get people's attention. I hadn't achieved much of anything professionally. I wasn't some self-made millionaire or critically acclaimed bestselling author. My one claim to fame was the fact that, as a teenager, I had been so concerningly obsessed with the World of Warcraft that I had become one of the highest-ranked players in the country. It made for a great story, but that was about it.

As a result, credibility wasn't something I started with. I had to earn it myself.

Luckily, how you build credibility on the internet is easy. In the simplest way, signals of credibility are nothing more than subtle (or not-so-subtle) signs that you know what you're talking about and are "worth" listening to.

There are three different layers of credibility.

The first layer is Implied Credibility.

You probably don't realize it, but whenever you consume something on the internet, it's really not the person you judge first.

It's the content.

Whether it's a video, an article, a song, etc., your very first judgment is whether or not the material itself resonates with you. This is how we discover new artists, new voices, new sources of information—and there's a feeling of excitement that comes with realizing, *after the fact,* that this thing you just stumbled upon is coming from someone you've never heard of before. You feel as though you just made an amazing discovery.

Implied Credibility is how much "Better" or "Worse" your content is than everyone else's *in your chosen category.* If someone comes across your article or song or video and it's *so much "Better"* than the vast majority of other creators in your category, they don't need to read your bio or take a look at your accolades to know whether or not you're someone credible. They've already made their judgement. Your content is *so good,* your credibility is implied.

Other signals of Implied Credibility are:

- **Profile picture:** Right out the gate, if your profile picture is blurry and half-hearted, what you're really telling readers is that you're not "playing the game" seriously—so then why should they take you seriously?

- **Bio:** "I like cats, coffee, and watching Netflix," is not an effective bio. Instead of trying to be clever, tell people who you are, what category your writing is in, and what makes you "credible."

- **Production quality:** If you post pictures, graphic designs, or videos within your writing, then the quality of these content types are going to speak for you. Low-quality images, for example, are going to tell readers you're operating on a shoestring budget.

High-quality images, on the other hand, lead readers to believe you have the means to hire a professional photographer (which means, "This person must be successful."). It's implied.

- **Grammar:** There is no faster way to lose credibility with a reader than to have writing littered with mistakes. (However, I too was once a 17-year-old blogger who didn't know the difference between 'their' and 'they're.') So while grammar mistakes can be an issue, don't let fear keep you from making progress as a writer. Just keep getting better as you go along.

- **Organization of thought:** If your writing reads smoothly, a reader is going to assume "you know what you're doing." If it's formatted well, they're going to assume "you've been writing for a while." These are subtle signals of credibility in the form of expertise.

- **Specificity:** Remember, Specificity Is The Secret. The more specific you are, the more likely a reader is going to immediately assume they are in the right place, reading the right writer for them.

This is what makes the "game" of online writing so fun.

A 23-year-old like me could wake up one day and decide to start playing the game. If I am capable of writing "As Good" or even "Better" than the best, most credible, most critically acclaimed writers *in my chosen category,* I can win. And I can win without spending a single penny on PR, advertising, or "credibility hacking."

The second layer is Perceived Credibility.

This is the layer of credibility 99% of people want for themselves.

They want to be able to say, "I've been featured in *Forbes*." They want to hack the Amazon algorithm so they can say they have a #1 best-selling book. They want to sign with a major publisher to be seen as "professional." They want to take a picture with Tony Robbins. They want a testimonial from Arianna Huffington. They want as many signals as possible to tell people, "I am an incredibly CREDIBLE person," with the hopes that *then* people will listen to what they have to say.

Now, the truth is, these signals do work. There's a reason why every company on earth has a banner on the front page of their site with a bunch of logos of major publications they've been mentioned in. There's a reason why every big-name book has one or two quotes on the front cover from other credible people (including this one). These signals can be extremely powerful in getting people's attention.

Other signals of Perceived Credibility are:

- **What credible people have to say about your writing:** "Nicolas Cole is the single greatest writer of this generation."
  –Abraham Lincoln

- **Which major publications your writing has appeared in:** "Featured in TIME, Forbes, Fortune, Business Insider, and many more."

- **How many followers you have on social media:** 100,000 followers sends a signal you simply cannot send with 100 followers.

- **High barrier-to-entry products:** Writing a book, or launching a high-production video course, are signals of credibility simply because they typically either require a significant amount of expertise and/or money in order to execute.

- **Badges and achievements:** #1 best-selling author on Amazon, *New York Times* best-selling author, *WSJ* best-selling author, Top Writer on Quora, Top Writer on Medium, LinkedIn Influencer, Verified on Instagram or Twitter, etc. These are all examples of badges and achievements that can be leveraged for Perceived Credibility.

- **How much money you've made from your craft:** Mystery novelist James Patterson is "The world's best-selling author. His total income over the past decade is estimated at $700 million." That's Perceived Credibility on a completely different level.

HOWEVER...

What so many people fail to realize is that these signals can also backfire—and they backfire often.

When you go to great lengths to acquire and leverage Perceived Credibility signals, you are making a promise to your readers. You're saying, "Look at all these people who think I'm credible. I *promise,* you won't be disappointed."

If you skip straight to this step in the game (and so, *so*, *so* many people do), chances are, every person whose attention you capture is going to be disappointed. They're going to know, within the first three paragraphs of reading your writing, whether or not they've been tricked. They're going to immediately measure what you're saying against what everyone else is saying *in your chosen category*. And if it's clear you aren't quite as compelling as you made yourself out to be, they aren't going to stick around.

You might have captured their attention—but you certainly didn't keep it.

The third layer is Earned Credibility.

This is the most undervalued form of credibility on the internet.

It's also the easiest to acquire.

Earned Credibility is nothing more than a signal of experience. The way I like to describe Earned Credibility is: imagine you stumble across someone's Instagram page. There's a clean profile picture. There's a great bio. And then there are four pictures, all posted from three years ago.

Immediately, you are going to think to yourself, "Ah, this is nobody." Their lack of effort, lack of consistency, and lack of content tells you everything you need to know about how seriously they're "playing the game."

Now, imagine you stumble onto someone's Instagram page and their most recent picture was posted 36 minutes ago. You keep scrolling, and you see content going back weeks, months, even years. When you scroll back to the top, you see this person has 6,000 followers. They aren't "Insta-famous," but they're certainly "playing the game" with intention.

You decide to follow.

Whether we realize it or not, the reason we choose to pay attention to some people and choose not to pay attention to other people is not because of Perceived Credibility. It's really not their fancy titles, badges of approval, or press logos that attract us into their vortex. It's actually their Implied Credibility (quality of content) and Earned Credibility (proof they're "playing and winning the game"). What hooks us is their consistency, their improvement over time, and most importantly, their ability to create something that resonates with us *in that particular category*. By "following" them, what we're really saying is *we believe what they create tomorrow will be "As Great" or "Better" than what they created today*—and we want to be there to experience it.

Other signals of Earned Credibility are:

- **How long you've been creating content for:** "Every day for 3 years" sends a very different signal than "I just started last week."

- **How often you create content:** "I write something new every day" vs "I write something every few months, when I feel like it."

- **How much content you've created:** "I have written more than 3,000 articles online" vs "I've written three blog posts."

- **How many people consume your content:** "I have more than 1,000,000 views on my writing" vs "I have 300 views on my writing."

- **How well one of your pieces of content has performed:** If one of your articles has thousands of Upvotes, Views, etc., that in itself is a badge of credibility—and clear proof what you have to say is valuable.

What's important to note here is that every single one of these forms of Earned Credibility can be acquired for free.

While Perceived Credibility can be bought—you can buy mentions in the press, you can buy followers on social media, you can buy testimonials, you can buy reviews, you can even pay people like me to ghostwrite a book for you—Earned Credibility can't be bought with money. As a result, there's something uniquely different that comes with these badges, in the sense that each is a reflection of *effort, skill, and self-discipline*. And in many ways, these types of badges actually send more powerful, more trustworthy signals to audience members than even the shiniest of more formal awards.

The secret is in how you choose to leverage them.

It took me a very long time to learn that nearly any sort of Earned Credibility badge or achievement can be leveraged up to the next. For example, when I was 25 years old and Quora named me one of their Top Writers for the year, very few people in the world had any idea what that meant. Being a Top Writer on Quora was a very big deal, but to anyone outside of Quora, that badge held insignificant Perceived value.

*What makes a badge of credibility valuable isn't really the badge itself. **It's how the writer chooses to wear it.***

As soon as I became a Top Writer on Quora (Earned Credibility), I started wearing that badge everywhere. I put "Top Writer on Quora" in all my bios on social media. I added the credential to the About page on my personal website. I even included the badge in my Quora answers, writing about how I became a Top Writer on Quora in the first place.

Since I was the one choosing to wear that badge of credibility proudly, other people started using that badge to describe "who I was" as a writer. When I spoke on podcasts, the host would introduce me as, "Nicolas Cole, a Top Writer on Quora." When my Quora answers started getting syndicated to major publications, they would add a line at the end of the piece: "Nicolas Cole, Top Writer on Quora." And remember, where they were getting that title from was from *my website, and my social media bios.* In 2015, most people didn't even know what being a Top Writer on Quora actually meant. But because I was wearing my badge proudly, everyone else took it upon themselves to be proud of my badge too.

This is one of the unspoken rules of building credibility on the internet.

Credibility is in the eye of the beholder—and it's a ladder anyone can climb.

The moment you have even one signal of Earned Credibility, you should start leveraging it. If one of your articles gets 10,000 views, you should have a link in your bio saying, "Read my most-popular article with more than

10,000 views." If something you write gets Tweeted by a prominent person in your industry, use that to your advantage: "Mark Cuban loved this article of mine—I think you will too." If you've been writing online for five years straight, why isn't that in your bio? "Writing every single day online since 2015. Read my most-popular articles here."

There are an infinite number of credibility signals that exist on the internet.

Unfortunately, most writers don't use these signals to their advantage. They have them, or they very easily could have them, they just choose not to leverage them.

As a result, they don't "appear" very credible at all.

Level 7: Create Your Own Category

Once you've made it through Levels 1 through 6, you will unlock the most important realization of your entire writing career.

Competing in other people's categories sucks.

It's actually very, very difficult to become the "Category King" of someone else's category. What I mean is, let's say you want to write horror stories. How are you ever going to be seen as "Better" at writing horror stories than Stephen King (no pun intended). Or let's say you want to write legal thrillers. How are you ever going to be seen as "Better" at writing legal thrillers than John Grisham? Or, here's a good one. Let's say you want to write a young adult fiction story about witchcraft and wizardry. HOW ARE YOU EVER GOING TO BE SEEN AS "BETTER" AT WRITING ABOUT A MAGIC SCHOOL FOR KIDS THAN J.K. ROWLING?

You're not.

You could get a few readers, maybe. You could even, one day, way down the road, become the second-best writer *in that specific category.* But the chances of you actually surpassing that "Category King," and being seen as "THE BEST" is highly unlikely.

So, what's a writer to do?

The answer is to create a new category of your own.

What I am about to share with you is the most under-discussed aspect of writing, and yet it is also the secret to why some writers miraculously "come out of nowhere" and become massive success stories—and others sound like the *same old, same old.*

Mega-successful writers (in both big ways, like selling millions of copies of books, and small ways, in going viral on the internet), don't *compete* within existing categories. What they do, *intuitively, accidentally, or intentionally,* is create a new category for themselves.

For example:

- **"Pop Science"**: Before Malcolm Gladwell, most non-fiction writers either wrote about science-backed material in a very formal, "high-falutin" sort of way, or they avoided the science altogether and just wrote general life advice. Gladwell, instead of competing in either of these two categories, created his own—which the media has since referred to as "Pop Science." His books are based on thorough research, but they're written for a non-academic audience.

- **"Wizardry For Kids"**: J.K. Rowling came almost fifty years after J.R.R Tolkien, and yet instead of trying to write a "Better" version of *The Lord Of The Rings*, she created a completely different category of "fantasy and magic" by writing a story intentionally aimed at younger readers.

- **"No-Bullshit Self-Help"**: The Self-Help industry over the years has been niched a gazillion different ways, but it wasn't until Jen Sincero published *You Are A Badass*, and Mark Manson published *The Subtle Art Of Not Giving A F*ck*, that a whole new niche emerged: telling people how to un-fuck their lives, plain and simple. All of a sudden, readers had to make a choice. Were they looking for a nice, calm, friendly self-help book (category), or were they looking for a no-bullshit guide to self-im-fucking-provement (new category)?

- **"Fratire"**: Before Tucker Max's, *I Hope They Serve Beer In Hell*, there was "satire," and there were fraternity stories told around bonfires while drinking Natty Light. And in the beginning, a lot of people misunderstood why Max's book series caught fire. Was it because they were funny? Yes. Were they well written? That's a subjective question. The real reason Max became a #1 *New York Times* best-selling author was because he had created a completely new category—and one no one else could enter without being immediately compared to Max and his debaucheries.

The list goes on and on.

Unfortunately, the vast majority of writers don't create their own categories. To be honest, most don't even know they can—let alone how.

Instead, what they do is they spend their entire lives trying to compete in someone else's category. From the moment they decide they want to become a writer, they look at someone else and think, "That's who I want to be." The irony is, in wanting to *be like* another writer, they trick themselves into playing a flawed game. They set out to try to be a "Better" version of a writer within an existing category, instead of creating a new and "DIFFERENT" category altogether.

As a result, they spend their entire writing career in someone else's shadow.

As writers, we all start out imitating each other, wanting to "be like" the person who inspired us to write. But at a certain point, once the fundamentals have been learned and the lessons have started to crystalize, a fork in the road presents itself. "Do I want to keep trying to be a 'Better' version of someone else? Or is it time I become a new and DIFFERENT version of myself?"

And DIFFERENT always beats "Better."

So, how do you create a category?

Categories are created at unlikely intersections, spotted by writers with an intimate understanding of one or multiple sub-categories.

There are a million different ways to create a category, but it's easiest to think about category creation as a matching game.

Your job as a writer—once you've found your strengths, your high-performing topic areas (validated by data), and where you prefer to sit on the Writing Spectrum—is to match different audiences, genres, and writing styles to create a new and DIFFERENT category.

- **AUDIENCE x GENRE:** Let's say you're a history buff, and you love writing historical fiction. The only problem is, adult historical fiction has a ton of competition. That's a massive category, and a tough one for you to compete in. So, leaving the genre the same, how can you adjust the AUDIENCE to make the genre something entirely new? An example of this would be: historical fiction *for kids*, or historical fiction *for war veterans*, or historical fiction *for immigrants*? These might sound like "small" categories, but remember, Specificity Is The Secret. By going all-in on a new and DIFFERENT category, you are forcing readers to make a choice. If you're a war vet and you love historical fiction that doesn't read like bubblegum but speaks in the lingo only a true war vet would understand, that genre is going to be your JAM.

- **GENRE x GENRE:** Take two genres that don't typically go together and all of a sudden you might have an interesting new category on your hands. What would it look like to combine the sci-fi genre with the memoir genre? Or what about the How To genre with the fiction genre? The more unexpected the pairing, the more likely it is for you to stumble onto something radically DIFFERENT and uniquely interesting.

- **AUDIENCE/GENRE x TONE:** In one category, where you sit on the Writing Spectrum could be expected and boring. But in a different category, it could be exciting and refreshing. Jen Sincero's, *You Are A Badass*, is a terrific example of how a tone shift created a whole new niche in the Self-Help category. (Ask most people, though, and they'll say, "The book was popular because it had a great title" or "It was really well written." They fail to see the category it created, and the choice it forced readers to make: "Do I want to read a self-help book that sounds warm and comforting? Or do I want to read a self-help book that slaps me in the face and tells me to wake the fuck up?").

Once you've created a new and DIFFERENT category in your mind, you must then communicate the differences of that category to your audience. This is what's called your "Point of View." Your POV is the way you see the world, the unique vantage point that allows everyone else to understand your perspective.

What is your new category and why is it different?

The idea here is to educate readers on how this new category is nothing like other nearby categories. One of my favorite examples here is the category of "military romance." Somewhere along the line, a writer woke up in the morning and thought, "You know, romance is a pretty big category. But I bet there are readers who only want to read romance novels in military settings." All of a sudden, you as a reader have to make a very concrete choice: do you want to read any romance novel? Or do you want to read a romance novel where the main character is in the military?

This is where, again, Specificity Is The Secret. The more specific you can be about why your new category is exactly what your target readers are looking for, the more likely it is readers will see this category of yours as unique and SEPARATE from any and all competition. Notice: I am not talking about your "brand" as a writer, or the title of your book, eBook, article, etc. I'm talking about marketing the defining characteristics of the category itself—leading readers to ask the most important question of all. "If this is the category I'm interested in, then who should I be reading? Who is the #1 writer here?"

And if you're the one who created and educated them on this new category, who are they going to see as the expert?

That's right.

You.

Chapter 4

Where You Should Be Writing Online—And Where You Should Not

The digital landscape is always changing.

Where you should be writing online today is not necessarily where you should be writing online tomorrow. In an attempt to make this book more "timeless" than "timely," I'm going to focus this chapter more on the *attributes* of where you should be writing online, more so than recommending tips and tricks that may work today but won't last forever.

At the beginning of this book, I defined Online Writing as *"...sharing **thoughts, stories, opinions, and insights** on a platform that already has an active audience."*

Most aspiring writers, industry thought leaders, business owners, consultants, public speakers, and digital marketers think this means writing for a major publication.

Why?

Because having a *Forbes* logo at the top of your article is instant Perceived Credibility.

And yes, while contributing to a major publication does have its benefits in the world of online writing, it's far from the "holy grail" people make it out to be. As someone who wrote for *Inc Magazine* for almost three years, and became one of their most popular writers, I want to pull back the curtain and debunk five myths about how much "exposure" publications really give their writers.

1. Writing for (or being featured in) a major publication does not automatically guarantee "millions of views."

People love data, so let me give you some data.

Of the 409 columns I wrote exclusively for *Inc Magazine*, only 44 of them exceeded 10,000 views in 2017.

- 28 of them were 10,000 to 19,000 views.

- 5 were 20,000 to 29,000 views.

- 4 were 30,000 to 39,000 views.

- 2 were 40,000 to 49,000 views.

- 2 were 50,000 to 59,000 views.

- 1 was 90,017 views.

- 1 was 128,041 views.

- And 1 was 133,000 views.

So, just because "all of *Inc Magazine*" gets 30 million views per month, does not mean your one article is going to get even a meaningful fraction of that.

Another unfortunate stat is that the average amount of

time a reader spends reading an article on a major publication is less than 60 seconds—with a 70-90% bounce rate (meaning once a reader starts reading an article on a major publication, less than 10% click to read a second).

This is because the vast majority of major publications monetize through advertising. Their entire model is to shove as many ads down the reader's throat before they run away. The name of the game is to then spend less on the cost of getting you to click than the profit generated on the ads shown to you within that sixty-second window.

As a result, publications are not built for prolonged reading experiences. Instead, they're optimized for SEO (articles that rank well in search results around industry specific keywords) or "clickbait" headlines that can grab people's attention on social media—either organically or via paid media. In all three of these scenarios, a user is discovering a single article, clicking to read, and then returning back to wherever they were before.

What all of this means is writing one single article guarantees almost nothing in terms of exposure. In fact, the majority of the traffic an article receives will be based on your sharing it on your own social media—with the primary benefit being your saying, "Check it out! I wrote something for *Forbes!*" and a handful of your Facebook friends and LinkedIn connections hitting Like and commenting congratulations.

2. When you write for a major publication, you don't have the freedom to write whatever it is you want to write about.

Think of yourself as an employee.

When major publications are looking for contributing writers or columnists, what they're really looking for is *volume within an under-resourced category.*

The real reason I landed my own column with *Inc Magazine* wasn't just because I was an effective writer. The reason was because, at the time, *Inc* was looking for more writers within their Creativity category. As I began writing for the site and bringing in hundreds of thousands of page views, sure, they allowed me to deviate from just writing about creativity—because I was clearly a net-positive writer for the publication. But every few months, I would hop on a call with my editor, and they would inevitably end up trying to steer me back into my lane, recommending topics they needed more writers covering.

I "worked" for them.

> If your goal is to write about the things you want to write about, **don't bother writing for a publication.**

When I started ghostwriting for executives—and I'm talking very, very successful business leaders; the kind who had brought companies public and/or exited for hundreds of millions of dollars—I helped many of them land columns of their own. And while you'd think that business and news publications would give people like this more freedom, they were still subject to the same scrutiny. I remember one editor telling this executive I had been working with for almost two years that one of his articles wasn't being objective enough. This was in 2018, when GDPR (General Data Protection Regulation) became enforceable in Europe and was having a dramatic impact on this guy's international business. The article we wrote together was about how companies needed to think about navigating this new law, and not get fined by the government.

But this editor wanted him to write as if he was a journalist, not a seasoned executive talking about his own business.

In order to keep his column, he had to play by their rules.

3. Writing for a major publication does not mean you get to promote yourself all day long.

The average column on a major publication receives less than 1,000 views.

Let me say that again:

The average column on a major publication receives less than 1,000 views.

The articles that "go viral" only fall into three categories:

- They are about an insanely successful company (Apple).

- They provide an unexpected perspective on a controversial and trending topic.

- They focus on personal development/life advice.

Out of my top 10 performing columns of 2017 for *Inc Magazine*, 9 had to do with personal development. The one that had to do with a company was about Facebook in the news.

I can't tell you how many authors, business owners, and public speakers think "if only" they could write for a major publication, then they would be able to promote their business or their book and all would be right in the world. What they don't take into consideration, however, is that people don't wake up in the morning excited to read about your best interests.

> **People read major publications for three reasons:** opinions, news, or to learn how to do something. That's it.

The fact that my top 10 highest-performing articles are predominantly about personal development should tell you something. These weren't articles about *me*—these were articles about *you*, the reader. These were pieces to get *you* thinking, to make *you* more productive, to help *your* life in some way. And it was because I was putting the reader first that my articles performed so well. Anytime I shifted the focus to myself, or leaned too heavily into my own "navel gazing," viewership fell.

All of my most popular Quora answers followed a similar methodology.

- 800,000+ views: How to become more confident.

- 783,000+ views: How to stop being average.

- 507,000+ views: What it feels like to go from unattractive to attractive.

- 425,000+ views: A stranger I met once that changed my life forever.

- 412,000+ views: Why having everything you want won't make you happy.

4. Social platforms will always exceed major publications in terms of reach.

There are times when articles on major publications will go viral and accumulate millions, tens of millions, even hundreds of millions of views.

But these are rare moments. And not only are they rare, but they usually don't favor thoughtful articles intended for a well-educated reader. The most viral articles for publications are pieces like, "No, Megyn Kelly Should Not Have Worn That Dress" (one of *Inc*'s most popular articles in all of 2016), or slideshow articles on Business Insider about Jeff Bezos's net worth measured in rice.

Social platforms, on the other hand, tend to be more generous to a wider range of writers.

Numbers alone tell the story. *Inc Magazine* averages around 30 million page views per month. Medium, a social writing platform, has somewhere around 30 million users—and Quora is about 10x the size of Medium, with 300 million users.

Side by side, my *Inc* column **never once outperformed my exposure on Quora or Medium.**

A really great month writing for *Inc Magazine*, I'd bring in 300,000 views.

On Medium though, 300,000 views in a month was considered average.

And between 2014 and 2018 on Quora, 300,000 views was considered a monumental failure. I consistently averaged over a million.

Even still today, my *Inc Magazine* reports tell me my 409 columns continue to generate around 80,000 views per month, passively. Meanwhile, my content on Medium and Quora together generates between 500,000 and 1,000,000 views per month passively.

Publications "seem" big, but in reality, their distribution is rather small.

5. On major publications, you don't "own" your own audience.

Finally, the biggest thing to think about before pledging your allegiance to a major publication is how much control you want over your content.

When you write for a publication, all your control goes out the window. Once an article goes live, it's not yours anymore—it belongs to the site. After a certain period of time (*Inc* requires a week, *Forbes* asks for two weeks, etc.), you're allowed to republish the article on your website, your blog, social media, etc., as long as you provide a link at the bottom stating, "This article was originally published on *Inc Magazine*."

In addition, very little is done for you (the contributing writer or columnist) to capture your readers. There is no "follow" button on your column. There is no mechanism for you to ask readers to type in their email and subscribe. Even the data most major publications give their writers is limited. At best, you'll know how many views an article received, and what the major referral traffic sources were (for example: *78% of readers came from Facebook*). But as far as demographic data, or engagement data, there really isn't any—and as a writer, this is the data you need to gather most.

As a contributing writer, your job is to produce page views for the publication. In return, **you get to leverage the name of the publication for your own Perceived Credibility.**

However, that's not to say there aren't benefits to contributing content to these major publications. Writing for *Inc Magazine* had a dramatic impact on my career as a writer. It gave me a different sort of credibility than Quora or Medium could, simply because there was a barrier to entry. "Not everyone" could contribute to *Inc*, which is what made it special.

Here are the benefits that come with contributing content to a major publication:

- **Perceived Credibility:** Once you write even one article for a publication, you can now say, "Published in...XYZ." You can place their logo on your website. You can use that one article as leverage to land more articles in more places. For example, I have only had two articles in *TIME*— and yet I can still say, "Published in *TIME*."

- **SEO:** Major publications have extremely high domain authority, meaning that if a page on

Inc Magazine or *Forbes* links to another website, that weighs heavily in Google's search algorithms. As an author, not only will both your column and bio link to your own personal or company website (telling Google it is credible and thereby pushing it up the rankings), but you can also find creative ways to link to your website(s) within your articles, further boosting your own SEO. If you want to see what this looks like in action, search "Nicolas Cole" into Google and you'll see I own the entire first 3+ pages of results. The reason is because I have hundreds of articles, across dozens of publications I've contributed to, all linking back to my personal website, my social platforms, etc.

- **Social Exposure:** For the last year of my writing for *Inc Magazine*, the biggest benefit I got out of my column was the fact that every time one of my articles went live, their Twitter account (with 2.7 million followers) would Tweet my latest article and tag me. Since I was writing 5+ columns per week, I was getting Tweeted by *Inc*'s Twitter constantly—which is how I built my own Twitter following of 7,500+ readers (many of whom are journalists, other columnists, business leaders, investors, marketers, writers, and so on). If you write often enough for a publication, and they regularly feature your work on their social profiles, this can be a powerful driver for your own audience growth. However, not every publication does this, and

9 times out of 10, they only promote their most popular contributing writers.

- **Money:** If you are a consistent writer looking for a side hustle, writing for a major publication isn't a bad pursuit. But in order to even be considered as a paid contributing writer, you need to 1) already have proven your ability to drive viewership elsewhere (I did this on Quora), 2) be a credible source of information in your chosen category, and 3) guarantee you can write a certain number of articles for the site per month. If you fall below that quota, you won't get paid. If you meet your quota or exceed it, most major publications will pay per page view and not per piece. This is in the best interest of the publication, in the sense that the writer only makes money if the publication makes money (since page views = ad revenue). However, in order to make any money at all using this model, you need to be authoring an obscene amount of content—or you need to get extremely lucky. Some months, I would write twenty-five or thirty articles and only make a few hundred dollars (which, divided by the number of hours spent writing, meant I was making far less than minimum wage), and other months, I would write a home-run viral article and get a check for $5,000. One of my closest friends, who I also helped land a column with *Inc*, wrote one of the publication's most viral articles of all time, accumulating more than

20,000,000 views in a single month. They had to cut him a check for $20,000, which he then used to buy a diamond ring and propose to his girlfriend (true story). If this sounds like the equivalent to winning the lottery, that's because it is. The vast majority of contributing writers don't get paid at all, simply because the volume they produce isn't enough to warrant paying them.

If you're a fiction writer, or a fitness writer, or any other type of writer, all these same rules apply. Even in the world of literature, short story publications play by very similar rules (just with less money at their disposal). Travel, food, and pop culture websites, same thing. All you need to know is that the primary benefit of writing for a publication is the Perceived Credibility that comes with it—and many, if not all of these sites use this to their advantage. You write for free, and in exchange you get to leverage their logo for your own credibility. And while the other benefits, such as SEO, social exposure, and money can certainly be nice, there are far better ways to achieve those same ends without having to play the role of "opinion journalist" for a publication or industry website.

Which is why I firmly believe the single best place to begin writing online is on some sort of social media platform.

The 5 Phases of Social Platforms— And Why Phase 3 Is Your Window of Opportunity

Before you can even begin entertaining the thought of writing for a major publication, let alone authoring a book, you still need to go through the steps of figuring out your category, discovering what makes your voice unique, and proving your writing has an audience.

In order to do these three things as quickly as possible, it's best to begin writing on a social media site that 1) already has a significant user base, 2) *is relevant to your chosen category*, and most importantly, 3) provides you with analytics into your target readers' behaviors. This is where writing on your own blog, or even someone else's website, falls short. The whole idea isn't to just hit publish and then pat yourself on the back. The idea is to hit publish and start gathering data. What are people Liking? What are people Upvoting? What are people Commenting? What are people Sharing?

These are the signals that will start to direct your writing style, and tell you whether you should go right or left.

Pros of writing on a social platform:

- Readers can easily discover you (whereas with a blog you are responsible for bringing the readers yourself, and with a publication you are hoping people will discover you via SEO and/or paid media).

- You can "earn" credibility with metrics like Views, Shares, Comments, Badges, Who-Follows-Who, etc.

- You can interact and build meaningful relationships with other writers and readers.

- You can build an audience, faster, in an environment that allows you to reach them quickly and effectively.

- You still "own" all of your content. Unlike writing for a major publication, you can do whatever you want with your content—including copy/pasting the exact same material onto different platforms.

- You are perceived differently. When someone reads your writing on your blog, it feels biased and subjective. When someone reads your writing on a social site, it feels more objective and "out in the open."

- Your content is more likely to be shared. Other websites and publications very rarely (if ever) syndicate or share content from someone's personal blog or company website. But content published in social environments is considered "fair game" and far more likely to be shared. Social platforms also have exponentially larger audiences than websites and publications, so when a piece of writing "catches fire" on a social site, it goes further, faster.

Cons of writing on social platforms:

- Feedback is much more immediate. (This is actually a pro, but for a lot of people it's seen as a con. They don't like the idea of writing in an environment that objectively tells them only one person Liked their article.)

- Criticism is more direct. Aspiring writers and industry leaders will avoid partaking in the social world online because they don't know how they'd handle a negative comment or someone disagreeing with what they wrote.

- "Anyone can write on social platforms." This is a criticism I've heard from high-status people who feel they are above sharing their insight on the same platform as a "nobody." These are the types of people who chase after contributing to major publications, almost exclusively because there is a barrier to entry and being allowed in makes them feel they are "where they should be."

My opinion is that all these cons are self-inflicted, and largely rooted in fear or insecurity.

Social platforms are fueling the next several generations of writers, thinkers, creatives, and industry leaders, period.

Here are the social platforms likely to remain relevant over the next five, and potentially the next ten years.

- **Quora:** I firmly believe Quora is the most undervalued social platform on the internet. With more than 300 million users and billions of page views every month, this is one of the lowest barrier to entry and highest reward websites for writers. Quora is great for How To writers, Life Advice writers, and non-fiction writers. I have written extensively about how to use this platform by authoring The Ultimate Guide To Quora on my website.

- **Medium:** The second generation of Blogger, the popular blogging website from the 2000s, Medium has become the best place to author opinion articles on the internet and build an audience for yourself as a columnist. You can gather data about who is reading your articles, what their interests are, etc. And you can tap into their ecosystem of 30M+ users. Medium caters to both fiction and non-fiction writers, however it caters dramatically more to non-fiction, opinion, and How To writers.

- **LinkedIn:** Most people don't think of LinkedIn as a publishing platform, but it is. Especially if you're looking to write business, productivity, technology, or news-related material, LinkedIn can be a powerful channel for extending your reach into these verticals and audiences. Again, why this platform is valuable at this point in time is because it allows writers to build an audience, gather data, and tap into the hundreds of millions of users already on the platform.

- **Wattpad:** For both fiction and non-fiction writers (although more so for fiction writers), Wattpad has become an incredibly powerful publishing platform. Here, anyone can begin publishing pages of their stories and books in real time. Readers can follow you and your stories, comment on them for other readers to see, and share your stories with their own friends. Wattpad has also created some undeniable success stories in the indie publishing world, like Anna Todd—a young writer who accumulated more than 1.5 billion (with a B) reads on Wattpad, leading to a publishing deal with Simon & Schuster. Her novel, *After*, went on to reach #1 on the *New York Times* best-seller list, was translated into 30+ languages, and was ultimately sold to Paramount Pictures for a movie adaption.

- **Twitter:** Years ago, I discovered a Twitter user by the name of @VeryShortStory. Every single tweet was an entire story arc in less than 140 characters. Sure enough, @VeryShortStory accumulated more than 100,000 followers, and eventually published a book titled *Very Short Stories*.

Thousands upon thousands of Twitter users have followed this same recipe: experiment with different niches, discover a voice that attracts an audience, and then eventually leverage that audience to launch a product and/or become an author.

- **Amazon:** Technically, Amazon checks off all our boxes (userbase, data, and ability to build an audience), it just may take you longer and cost you a bit more time and money in order to discover what's working and what's not. My personal belief is that it's easier, more efficient, and more effective over the long term if you start writing shorter form content on social platforms (like the ones listed above) and *then* publish proven material on Amazon. However, there are enough success stories of independent writers finding success exclusively on Amazon that it's worth acknowledging the viability of this path from a self-published author's perspective.

Here's why I wouldn't get too married to any one of these platforms.

Every single website on the internet, social media platforms included, has a limited lifespan.

Some websites, publications, and social media platforms last a few years. Some last a decade. A rare few last beyond that—and for those still standing, either the opportunity to capitalize has passed or you were one of the select few users who rose to the top and you're still reaping your rewards. YouTube, although not a writing platform, is a terrific example. Trying to become a popular YouTuber today is much more difficult than it was 10 years ago. We're seeing the same thing happen in 2020 with podcasts on Apple and Spotify. It's much harder to start a popular podcast today than it was five years ago. Is it impossible? Certainly not. It's just worth acknowledging where in the life cycle each platform is when you begin.

The life cycle tends to look something like this:

Phase 1: New website or platform is invented—early audiences flock.

This is going to be a crash course in entrepreneurship and early-stage investing.

The overwhelming pro to "starting early" on an emerging platform is that as the platform grows, so do you. In fact, many early-stage websites and social platforms will go above and beyond to empower their early users and content creators, because without *you* the site ceases to hold value. People don't spend time on platforms that don't have content they want to consume.

The con, however, is that you are banking on the platform's success in order to remain relevant. The earlier a platform is in its life cycle, the riskier an investment it is (for investors, but also for content creators). You could invest a significant amount of time, energy, and resources in bringing your audience from one platform over to this new platform, only for the new platform to suddenly fail, go out of business, or get shut down. This is the argument 99% of people make for why you shouldn't start writing on a social platform, and why you should start a blog instead.

I want to clarify here I'm not advocating for going all-in on emerging, high-risk social platforms. I'm advocating for targeting slightly more established (or very established) social platforms, where a lot of things would need to go wrong for the company and website to fail.

Phase 2: Website or platform starts gaining traction—early users become "influencers."

The turning point for most emerging platforms is the point at which early users start becoming "internet celebrities" that represent the platform.

This has happened on every single social platform in history. YouTube gave rise to "YouTubers." Instagram power-users became "Instagram influencers." Whenever a platform starts growing exponentially and popular content creators begin to separate themselves from the pack, the "game" is unveiled to the general public. Suddenly, anyone new to the platform realizes there is a hierarchy, a ladder they can climb—and if they are willing to "play the game," they can build an audience for themselves too.

By the time this happens, the website or social platform is likely to be heavily funded. In Phase 1, a newer platform might have raised anywhere from a few hundred thousand dollars to a few million dollars in order to gain initial traction. By Phase 2, funding is likely closer to $30-50 million. For example, Instagram raised $50 million at a $500 million valuation in its Series B. Quora raised the exact same amount at a $400 million valuation.

At this point, the likelihood of a platform "failing" becomes dramatically lower. Venture capitalists and seasoned investors don't just watch a company valued at $500 million vanish into thin air, no matter how many worst-case scenario events happen. This means, even if you invested a year or two into building your profile and content library on a platform in phase 2, you would still have plenty of time to move your audience and content elsewhere before the platform went under.

Again, the likelihood of this happening is extremely small. But since so many people choose blogging over writing on social platforms for this exact reason, it's important to understand the flaws in this thinking.

Phase 3: Website or platform is established and begins a decade-long journey to profitability.

This was the phase Quora was in when I started writing on the platform in 2014.

For context, Quora had raised its $50 million Series B two years prior, in 2012. Raising $50 million meant the platform was signing itself up for a decade-long journey to slowly convert its free platform and users into an advertising revenue generating machine. By the time I joined the platform, a small number of power-users had already been crowned as Top Writers, and the hierarchy had been established. It was also clear Quora wanted to continue rewarding these Top Writers, since they were responsible for engaging the platform's community and writing high-quality content for the site.

In hindsight, I joined Quora at the perfect time.

I was early enough in the sense that the hierarchy had only recently been established, but late enough to have confidence that time invested on this platform wouldn't be for nothing. Quora was clearly growing fast, and the platform would be alive for at least another five years—maybe even more than a decade. Seeing both of these qualities is what made me feel comfortable beginning to build myself there, and make Quora my primary writing platform.

Whenever I look for new platforms to leverage as a writer, this is the "window" I look for. Because this "window" provides maximum upside for content creators.

The reason is because as soon as a platform reaches this stage, it needs to achieve certain exposure and engagement metrics in order to warrant turning on its advertising machine. In 2014, when I started writing on Quora, ads on the site didn't exist yet—and over the next few years, they only existed in beta form to a very small number of test clients.

What these social platforms then do is begin prioritizing their high-volume and high-engagement content creators, giving them more and more exposure in user feeds—because they want to ensure engagement metrics remain high. In addition, because there isn't any advertising on the site or in-feed yet, there is dramatically less friction between you and the people who follow you. Back then, if I wrote something on Quora, there was a good chance nearly every single person who followed me saw it.

As the years went on, this was no longer the case.

Phase 4: Advertising model is launched and user reach starts falling.

As soon as advertising begins on a platform, you can expect your reach to fall.

Most people don't know why this happens, so let me explain.

When a platform monetizes with ads, what happens is they have to start picking and choosing which content to show users in their feeds. Without ads, you might have seen 20 potential pieces of content in the three minutes you spent scrolling. But with ads, you might only see 15 pieces of content, with 5 ads sprinkled in. Well, where did the other 5 pieces of content go? They're still somewhere on the site, they're just not being prioritized—which means those content creators are getting less views.

This is what's known as "throttling." The platform begins to withhold your reach as a content creator, forcing you to spend money in order to receive the same amount of exposure you used to receive organically. Facebook invented this model, and it's the reason why less than 3% of all your Facebook fans see any of the content you post on the platform—unless you spend money to "Boost" it.

The exposure I received on my Quora answers in 2015 was significantly higher than the exposure I received in 2018, 2019, and so on. That's because I was in "the window" where the platform was growing like crazy, but hadn't yet started throttling user reach and adding ads into the mix. By 2018, that window had passed, and even though I was still averaging hundreds of thousands of views on my content, it was a fraction of what I had been averaging just two years prior.

Now, this isn't necessarily a bad thing, and your reaction shouldn't be, "That's so unfair!"

The reality is, these social platforms need to find a way to make money, and this is one of the only models (thus far) with any sort of proven success. Otherwise, all our favorite social platforms would require a monthly subscription to be ad-free (like Netflix).

Second, once a platform incorporates advertising revenue (or moves to a subscription model, like Medium has), this usually means mechanisms are being launched to pay and reward content creators as well. For example, YouTube launching ads meant YouTubers could monetize their channels. Instagram launching ads meant you could build your audience on Instagram, boost certain posts, and drive traffic to a site where you were selling a product. Medium moving to a subscription and paywall model meant writers could earn money based on how many views their pieces behind Medium's paywall generated.

The name of the game is understanding where a platform is in its lifecycle, so that you can take maximum advantage of its current state.

Phase 5: Business model is established, reach is throttled, and it's time to find a new platform.

Once a social platform has fully integrated advertising into its model, organic reach will only continue to decline.

If you started investing in a platform early, or joined at a time where you were able to climb the ranks and become one of its power users, then you will forever have an advantage over other, newer users. For example, I contribute new content to Quora far less now than I did in 2015. However, my audience is still intact, meaning my organic exposure is going to be dramatically higher than someone who is just starting on the platform today. That said, every few years a new "class" of power-users emerges across all social platforms. Either previous power-users reached their goals and plateaued, got burned out and quit, or decided to move on to a new platform. So while you will maintain an advantage, you won't stay "king of the hill" forever and ever.

At this point, you have two options.

As a writer, you can either continue investing all of your time into your original platform, and if the platform is providing you with enough upside (reach is still great, audience is still growing, and content is still generating a profit—either directly via products or indirectly via exposure), then you should stay put. Or, you can diversify, and start moving your audience somewhere else. Ideally, you would want to move them to the next platform you see entering its own Phase 2 or Phase 3, providing you with a new window of opportunity for rampant growth.

For example:

- If you remember all those success stories of Amazon self-published authors selling hundreds of thousands of copies of eBooks in the late 2000s, that's because Amazon was in its "window" of opportunity for self-published authors. It's still possible today, it's just harder, more expensive, with far more competition.

- If you remember how brands were willing to pay obscene amounts of money for campaigns with Instagram influencers between 2012 and 2016, that's because Instagram was in its "window" of opportunity for influencers. By 2017, supply had increased, demand had decreased, and "Influencer Marketing" (although still tremendously popular) had lost its allure. You can still make money as a social media influencer today, there's just more competition.

- If you remember when Musical.ly started turning teenagers into lip-sync superstars in 2016, that's because the platform had entered its "window" of opportunity for a new form of content creators. A year later, it was acquired by TikTok, and creators who had invested during that "window" of growth suddenly saw an insane increase in exposure over the following three years. By 2019, TikTok had started beta testing in-feed ads, signaling the platform had officially entered Phase 4.

As you can see, this lifecycle occurs on *all types* of social platforms.

This is what I mean when I say, whichever platform is "where you should be writing" today, won't necessarily be "where you should be writing" tomorrow. For example, Medium launched in 2012, and I didn't start writing there until 2017. Why? Because the platform hadn't matured enough yet.

In Phase 1 and 2, Medium was extremely small, niche, and invite-only—primarily focusing on attracting high-level journalism talent. Around 2014 was when the site started to open up and attract more "everyday" writers. And by 2015, the company had raised $57 million in Series B, followed by another $50 million in Series C a year after. The "window" of opportunity had begun, and as a writer, I felt confident that time invested in the platform wouldn't go to waste.

I was right.

Between 2017 and today, I have accumulated more than 55,000 followers on the platform, and generated more than 20,000,000 views on my writing on Medium alone. The important nuance here is that I have written very little *new* material on Medium—55,000 followers and 20 million views have come as a result of simply republishing all my old Quora content, as well as my 409 *Inc Magazine* columns (crediting the publication at the bottom of each post, of course) on a daily basis.

In addition, when Medium launched its paid program in 2018, incentivizing writers to publish their writing behind the platform's paywall, I started republishing all my old content behind their paywall. "Maybe this will be like earning royalties on work I've already written," I thought. Nobody said I could or couldn't do this—I just decided to test the rules of the game on my own. To date, I've generated close to $100,000 from Medium alone (averaging $2,500 to $5,000 per month), all from republishing old content.

Will this last forever?

Maybe. Maybe not.

Of all writing platforms today, Medium is one of the most uncertain. The company has raised $137 million, been around for almost a decade, and still isn't profitable. That said, the CEO is Ev Williams, who was the former co-founder and CEO of Twitter. So again, Medium isn't going to just vanish into thin air. However, it's worth remaining conscious of where platforms like Medium are in their lifecycles, so that you can make conscious decisions about where you want to invest your time, energy, and resources.

> When it comes to writing online, platforms will always change, **but the rules will stay (pretty much) the same.**

For example, the next writing platform I am paying close attention to these days is Substack.

Substack is aiming to be the "social" writing platform for paid newsletters. The reason I say "social" is because, unlike true social platforms where the purpose is to browse and scroll, Substack actually operates much closer to a tool for writers rather than a social environment (in the sense that there isn't an algorithmic feed where you can consume new content, follow writers, etc.). However, the fact that they allow users to loosely browse newsletter creators tells me the social component of their site will develop over time.

Substack is still in Phase 1.

In 2019, the platform raised $15.3 million from one of the most well-known venture capital firms in Silicon Valley—Andreesen Horowitz (a16z). This means some very smart people are betting on the growth of the category of "paid newsletters" for writers and media creators. If this category continues to grow, and Substack is the creator of this category, then you better believe the platform is going to grow exponentially over the next five plus years.

For this reason, I've already moved my own newsletter over to Substack.

Chapter 5

How Writing On Social Platforms Works (And How To Not Give Up)

Deciding to start writing online is one thing.

Not giving up is entirely another.

The unfortunate reality is that most of us suffer from "instant gratification syndrome." As soon as we start something new, we want to know we're amazing at it, that the world loves us, and all we could have ever desired is about to come barreling forth. The number of people who have said to me, "I just wrote my first article online, but I only got 37 views so I don't know if it's really working," would shock you.

The truth is, *nobody*, not even the most talented writers on earth, show up to a brand-new platform, write one single article, and experience overnight success. There is no such thing as, "I wrote my first piece and received 10 million views." If that's your expectation, get it out of your head now.

Second, and I'm going to be brutally honest with you here, unless you really love the craft and process of writing, the path to becoming an independent, successful, widely read writer on the internet is going to frustrate the absolute shit out of you. Writing online requires an unrelenting commitment to consistency. Writing online means tolerating the fact that pieces you spend hours slaving over are going to go unnoticed, while pieces you write in twenty minutes are going to land on the front page of Reddit and go viral (which is what happened to me). On top of that, writing online (and the onslaught of feedback you will receive, both positive and negative) is not for the faint of heart. One of the very first comments I received on one of my earliest blogs as a teenager was, "This wasn't worth reading, and you're a terrible writer. I hope you get hit by a bus on your way to school." How 17-year-old me internalized that as positive motivation, I'll never know.

HOWEVER...

Mastering the art of online writing is also incredibly rewarding.

By learning how to use your voice, how to create your own category, and how to market yourself, your words, your books, and yourself as a brand, you will have far more leverage than 99% of writers out there.

And leverage means freedom.

If your goal is to be a successful writer, **then social platforms are for publishing first, and consuming second.**

I have a rule I live by, and it goes like this:

"The number of hours I spend consuming should never equal or exceed the number of hours I spend creating."

One of the biggest mistakes aspiring writers make is they spend hours and hours scrolling through social platforms and websites, looking at other writers and asking themselves who they're supposed to "be." This habit eventually evolves into an obsession with trying to find "the answer" by consuming other writers—instead of investing that time into exploring themselves.

The purpose of writing on social platforms and "Practicing in Public" is not to read. I don't care what famous author or literature teacher said that in order to become a great writer, you have to read. Yes, that's true. But there should be an asterisk that clarifies that stupid phrase and says, *BUT, the number of hours you spend consuming should never equal or exceed the number of hours you spend creating.* You don't become a writer by reading other writers.

You become a writer by writing—a lot.

When you start writing on a social platform, your goal is to "beat the game." In order to beat the game, you need to actually *play* the game, get feedback from the game, and internalize that feedback to change your strategies over time and make your way up the ladder—in whatever form that means to you. The more you write, the more data you will accumulate, the better your skills will get, the faster you will learn. Conversely, the less you write, the less data you will accumulate, the longer it will take for your skills to improve, the slower you will learn.

In order to set expectations properly, let's walk through the different stages of growth you will experience when writing on a social platform.

Stage 1: Just Start Writing

It doesn't matter who you are—a recent college graduate

with big dreams of becoming the next James Patterson, or the retired CEO of a publicly traded company—the first thing you write and publish on the internet is going to give you anxiety.

There's a lot of pressure that comes with writing online. "What will people think? Am I doing it right? What if someone disagrees with me? Will I even like what I wrote a few months from now?" After more than a decade of confronting these same questions in myself, as well as talking hundreds and hundreds of other writers (and clients) off this very same ledge, what I've ultimately concluded as being the underlying fear, the "root of the root," is fear of regret.

We are afraid of sharing who we are today—because we believe who we'll be tomorrow will be "better."

This is a vicious cycle.

Part of getting started writing online means acknowledging that whatever it is you publish today will not be the single greatest thing you ever write. In fact, if it was, I'd make the argument you have an even worse problem on your hands. Instead of getting better over time, you're going to get worse.

On April 11, 2014, I wrote my very first answer on Quora.

Here it is, in all its glory:

Is Elite Daily a legitimate site? Why?

I was a contributing writer for Elite Daily a while back---which probably isn't the best thing to admit with my following opinion:

The site does a great job at making you think what you're reading is well-informed and worthwhile, but the truth is, a lot of the writers are kids no older than you (if you're in the 20-26 demographic) and are merely sharing their opinions. Nothing wrong with that. I was one of them, and if they're good enough writers, the content can be entertaining and even somewhat knowledgable. Seeing as the news these days is hardly worth the title "professional" anyway, Elite Daily can be a great resource for someone looking for quick news or a nice list of 10 reasons why they shouldn't be in a committed relationship at 22 years old. But should you read Elite Daily hoping to have the mental whip of someone who reads Harvard Business Review or Chicago Booth's Capital Ideas? No. No you should not. That'd be like reading Buzz-feed and wondering why your ACT score isn't improving.

Elite Daily on Twitter is nice because they keep you informed about pop culture. Beyond that, it is barely a college-level newspaper.

End scene.

If it's not blindingly obvious, my writing style has evolved significantly since that first Quora answer—and that answer was a 10x improvement compared to my gaming blogs as a teenager. I don't write with those same rhythms anymore. I don't use rapid-fire metaphors, or have that same underlying sarcastic tone. Yet, that's where I was in my life when I wrote that. I was 24 years old. I was trying to "prove" I knew how to write. And on that day, in that one Quora answer, I captured "me" in that moment of time.

Looking back at it now, I don't feel regret.

What I feel is astonishment at how much I've improved—and thankfulness I had the guts to begin the journey of practicing my craft.

Every time I've started writing on a new platform online, I've found the beginning pattern to look something like this:

Post #1: "Hello! Thank you for having me. It's truly an honor for me to be here, internet."

Post #2: "Alright look, here's the real deal. I'm going to give it to you straight."

Post #3: "What is life, what am I doing here, and does any of this even matter?"

Right around Post #4 is where the first real checkpoint kicks in. The novelty of starting something new wears off, data begins revealing the truth of the situation—"I'm not an overnight success story, what?"—and subconsciously there is a realization that any and all success will be the product of hard work.

This is where the vast majority of people give up.

Stage 2: Write Consistently For 6 Months And *Then* Make A Decision

The writers who become successful aren't necessarily the most talented writers.

The writers who become successful are the most *consistent* writers.

It's impossible to know whether or not you have something meaningful to say, or if a platform is worth writing on, unless you give yourself six months to find out. When my co-founder and I started Digital Press, ghostwriting on behalf of busy founders and executives, we required them to sign six-month contracts for our service—not because we wanted to guarantee longer term revenue (although, that too), but because it would have been impossible to judge the value we were providing in thirty or sixty days. Truthfully, even six months is a hyper-condensed time-frame—but it's usually enough time to get some sense as to what's working and what isn't.

In the first six months of writing anywhere social on the internet, you have three primary goals:

Goal #1: See whether or not you can be consistent.

Nothing else matters unless you are writing on a regular basis.

Growth hacks, social media strategies, "viral tactics," none of it can be applied to your writing unless you're *actively writing in the first place.*

If you are publishing once every two months, or once every six months, then you should not have any expectations for the performance of your writing. Don't be surprised if nobody follows you. Don't be upset if you don't "rise up the ranks" on any of the platforms. Realize you are treating writing as a hobby, which means you are not actively playing (and competing within) "the game."

The minimum amount you should be writing and publishing new material online is once per month. That is the absolute minimum. The people who can get away with this cadence are executives, speakers, authors, investors, and working professionals who have already made strides building themselves on the internet. These are people who are further along in their careers, and have built an engaged network on LinkedIn or a buzzy following on Twitter. It's very rare that someone with absolutely zero digital footprint (regardless of how successful or well-known you are in the real world) starts writing online and immediately commands attention.

My true "recommended minimum" however is to publish something once every other week.

> In order to be taken seriously on the internet as an authority in your category and a leader in your industry, niche, or genre, **you need to be writing and publishing new material 2x per month.**

Going back to what we talked about earlier in this book, the reason people choose to "follow" writers online in the first place is because they are looking for a credible source of information within a particular category.

Seeing that someone publishes new information once per month, or once every few months, doesn't typically satisfy our wants as audience members. But if you come across someone publishing new material a few times a month, or better yet, every week, you'll be much more likely to follow them and have a reason to pay attention. And if you *really* want to beat the game of capturing and keeping attention, if you truly want the most guaranteed path to success, then you need to be writing and publishing something new several times per week—or ideally, every single day.

There are a few reasons why.

First, think of a social media algorithm as a roulette wheel. The more times you spin the wheel, the more chances you have of winning. Every time you create a new piece of content, you are pushing that content into the social platform's algorithm and "spinning the wheel." If you are only writing and publishing once per month, you are only spinning the wheel once every thirty days. But if you're writing and publishing every single day, you're spinning the wheel thirty times in thirty days. Compound this over the course of six months, and the former is only getting to play the game six times, while the latter is getting to play the game 180 times. Who do you think is going to win more often?

Second, readers are fickle. So are viewers, listeners, and consumers of any type of content. We are developing more and more into a world of instant gratification. If my favorite content creator stops playing the game, I'm not going to sit around and wait for them to come back. I'm going to find someone new to pay attention to. For this reason alone, you have to understand that in order to be "seen" as a credible, consistent source of information, you need to prove to audience members you're going to be there for them and with them, day in and day out.

Third, you have no idea which one of your creations is going to be "the one" that takes off. Just a few months before starting this book, I was trying to decide which article of mine to republish on Medium that day. I took a look through my library and found this short post about relationships I had written fairly quickly almost a year prior. "Eh, nobody really liked this article on Quora, I doubt it'll do very well on Medium," I thought. Still, I didn't know what else to publish, so I threw it on Medium anyway. Within an hour, it started going viral, and by the end of the day it had become one of my most-popular Medium articles of all time, racking up more than 200,000 views and 20,000 Claps. This exact situation has happened to me more times than I can count—and what I've learned is, I don't know which of my pieces are going to perform the best, and you don't either. All that matters is whether or not we keep spinning the wheel and playing the game.

Goal #2: Start gathering data about what your most popular categories are.

In your first six months of writing online, you should be less concerned with "establishing" yourself and more focused on "discovering" yourself.

The way we would engineer this process for our clients at Digital Press is we would come up with three categories ("Content Buckets") that represented who they were and what they wanted to write about. One category might be their industry (Biotech), the second might be related to their position within their company (Marketing), and the third might be a personal interest (Mountain Biking & Self-Discipline).

We would then begin writing and publishing content in all three of these different categories, alternating back and forth until we started to see patterns emerge. We were running an experiment. And what we usually found was, the topics they *thought* people would want to hear about from them weren't actually the topics data told us were most engaging. In this example, these were the buckets of a client of ours who is the CEO of a publicly traded bio-tech company. Turns out, his most popular articles weren't academic takes on the biotech industry. His most popular articles were stories about the mountain biking trips he would take with his friends, and the lessons he learned about self-discipline in the process.

Once you start gathering data about what's working and what isn't, you now have a decision to make.

If you start writing about marketing strategies, but data tells you it's your stories about being an angel investor people love reading most, you should pay attention to that. If you start writing sci-fi, but you discover it's actually your historical fiction people are flocking to, data is trying to tell you something. If you start writing poetry, but you find your morning meditations are what get dozens of people to comment and engage with your writing, what are you going to do? Keep writing poetry?

Once data enters the equation, this is where the "Who Do I Want To Be?" conversation gets interesting. Do you want to keep writing what you had originally wanted to write about? Or do you want to write what people clearly want more of?

My answer is: you should always do both.

> Data doesn't lie. But data is also a reflection of the external crowd, **and not necessarily your internal compass.**

If all you want is to climb the ladder as fast as possible and collect as many external achievements as you can (badges, awards, money, etc.), then follow the data and do nothing else. If what the world wants from you is life lessons, then give them life lessons. Let data tell you your next move, give people exactly what they want, and win the game.

On the flipside, if you don't really care what the outcome is (people say this is what they want but then get frustrated when nobody reads their writing), then ignore the data. Live your life, write your poetry, and satisfy your soul.

However, I believe (and have discovered for myself) there is a third option, and that's *to optimize the former so you can introduce people to the latter.* For example, I recently wrote a book of poetry called *Slow Down, Wake Up,* and started sharing more of my poems on social platforms like Quora, Medium, and Twitter. I like writing poetry. I've been writing poetry for more than a decade. Instead of ignoring this "content bucket" in my library completely, I've leveraged my *proven* writing to bring attention to my *passion* writing. I let data tell me what people want to hear from me most, and leverage that data to "win the game," while still keeping my own personal projects as a priority.

This book you're reading is a perfect example.

A lot of people follow me on Quora, Medium, Twitter, and Instagram because of the writing advice I share. Data tells me this is one of my high performing "content buckets." But within this book, I just told you about a poetry book I wrote called *Slow Down, Wake Up.* If you enjoy me as a writer, maybe you'll check it out.

I'm not pretending my poetry doesn't exist.

I'm giving you both—while also understanding which topic area is the priority for most of my readers.

Goal #3: Pay close attention to writers at the top of the hierarchy of the social platform—and constantly measure yourself against their performance.

People make "the game" of social media so much more complicated than it really is.

If you want to surpass even the most popular, highest-performing writers *within an existing category*, all you have to do is everything they're doing, more consistently.

- If they publish new material 7 days per week, you need to publish new material 7 days per week.

- If they write 3,000+ word stories, you should write 3,000+ word stories.

- If they interview industry titans and summarize their takeaways, you should interview industry titans and summarize their takeaways.

- If they encourage readers to Tweet them with questions and ideas, you should encourage readers to Tweet you with questions and ideas. And if they respond to every single Tweet that comes their way, you should respond to every single Tweet that comes your way.

- Etc.

Your job is to study the competition and understand exactly why they are succeeding in the first place.

If they title their articles in all caps, why are they doing that? Was there a point in time when they weren't doing that? What happened to their engagement once they started doing that? Have their Likes, Comments, Views, etc., increased since then?

If they make each sentence of their post its own paragraph, why are they doing that? What's the effect it has on you, the reader? Was there a point in time when they weren't doing that? What happened to their engagement once they started doing that?

If they post a high-quality photo at the top of every article, why are they doing that? What do you think they're trying to achieve? Was there a point in time when they weren't doing that? What happened to their engagement once they started doing that?

Question everything. Nothing a creator does repeatedly is accidental.

The creator might not be fully conscious of how or why they decided to start using shorter paragraphs, or why they intuitively stopped using as many sub-heads, but if it's a pattern that means something about it is working. It's your job to spot those patterns, mimic them, and then slowly shape them into your own style.

For example, if you wanted to "beat me" at the game of online writing, and acquire all the achievements I've acquired, all you would need to do is:

- Publish something new every single day (because I publish something new every single day).

- Write fast-paced articles that use short paragraphs, declarative language, and subheads for every main point.

- Combine actionable advice for the reader with personal stories from your own life that illustrate how you gained the insight you're sharing in the first place.

- Collaborate with professional photographers, build your personal brand, and attach pictures of yourself with the articles you write.

- Publish more than 3,000 articles online over the next five years.

- Contribute dozens of articles to *Inc Magazine, Forbes, Harvard Business Review, Fortune, Business Insider, The Chicago Tribune, The Huffington Post, TIME,* and more, to build your Perceived Credibility.

- Land a few speaking gigs, and capture pictures of you speaking to illustrate more Perceived Credibility.

- Speak on 100+ different podcasts, illustrating even more Perceived Credibility.

- Etc.

What a lot of people don't realize is that each one of these "achievements" is nothing more than a step along the journey. Just one single step. When I first started playing "the game," these were the steps I realized other writers (the writers I wanted to be like and surpass) had taken themselves. My first week on Quora, I quickly saw that all the top writers were publishing something new every day—which meant, if I wanted to be like them, I needed to publish something new every day too. And all of them wrote in this fast-paced style that never forced the reader to slog through a long, boring paragraph—which meant, if I wanted to engage with audience members the same way, I needed to write in that fast-paced style too. And all of them had found a way to get some of their articles republished in major publications like *TIME, Forbes, Business Insider*, etc.—which meant I needed to find a way to get some of my articles republished in those major publications too.

These unspoken "rules of the game" exist on every single platform.

All the most-popular Twitter writers share things in common. All the most-popular YouTubers share things in common. All the most-popular Medium writers share things in common. All the most-popular Quora writers share things in common.

Your job is to find the common threads, make them part of your own strategy, and then slowly over time create a style and category of your own.

Stage 3: Once You've Proven You Can Be Consistent, Pour Some Gasoline On Your Fire And Go KABOOM!

If you can make it through Stage 1 and 2, chances are, you'll start to see a very clear path forward for yourself as a writer.

However, if you're unable to be consistent for six months, if you're incapable (no matter how hard you try) to write on a regular basis, I have some bad news for you:

You're not a writer.

I'm intentionally being blunt here because if you struggle with self-doubt, then I really want this point to sink in. Being a writer is not a destination. There isn't a point on the road at which you are, *officially*, someone worth following on the internet. Attention has to be earned, engagement has to be nurtured, and most of all, relevancy has to be maintained. Which means, if you truly want writing to be part of your life or career, then "being a writer" isn't actually your goal. Your goal is to *write* (ACTION)— and it's *through writing* that you will BE "a writer."

So, if you can't be consistent for six months, either realize you love the idea of being seen as a writer more than you love sitting down and writing and move on to something else, OR, try again.

Pinpoint your mistakes.

Be honest about why you weren't able to remain consistent.

Confront some fears, get back on the horse, and start writing again TODAY.

> **Consistent output is the secret** to every growth metric on the internet: Views, Comments, Likes, Shares, etc.

Once you have a sound foundation as a consistent writer on the internet, now you can begin adding in all the fun growth strategies that start to separate amateur writers from professional writers.

Here are some of my favorite, all of which remain true no matter which platform(s) you choose:

Audience Hacking

Audience Hacking means collaborating with another writer who has a similar audience to you—introducing your audience to them and their audience to you. The reason I encourage you to target writers with a similar sized audience though is because it's unlikely you're going to get someone with 10x more followers to want to power-level you—but people who are around your level tend to see it as an even trade. This writer could be *within your chosen category*, however I would actually encourage you to find ways to collaborate with writers outside of your category as well—so you can widen your net.

Collaborations could include:

- Co-authoring an article together

- You interviewing them, and them interviewing you

- You sharing one of their articles, them sharing one of your articles

- You both meeting up in real life, taking a picture or shooting a short video clip together, posting it and tagging each other

- You giving them a testimonial, and them giving you a testimonial

- Basically you both creating or sharing content of any kind together, and sharing it with your respective audiences

For example: the testimonial on the cover of this book is from Dr. Benjamin Hardy. Ben became the #1 most-read writer on Medium right around the same time I became the #1 most-read writer on Quora. We were connected through a mutual friend, and because we had both climbed up our respective ranks in very similar ways, we became friends too. As I was getting ready to publish this book, I thought, "What writers around my level would be willing to collaborate?" I reached out to him, and he offered to give me a testimonial for my book if I gave him a testimonial for his.

Audience Hacking is extremely common in every industry. When a *New York Times* best-selling book has a testimonial on the cover from another *NYT* best-selling author, that's Audience Hacking. When one podcaster interviews another well-known podcaster, that's Audience Hacking. When a popular fashion YouTuber makes a video with a popular cosmetics YouTuber, that's Audience Hacking. When Justin Bieber makes a song with Ariana Grande, that's Audience Hacking.

It's an incredibly effective way to market yourself to new audiences while at the same time creating content that is different and maybe even better than what you could otherwise create on your own.

Trend Jacking

Trend Jacking is probably the easiest, most common growth hack on the internet.

Whenever something big happens in the news, it becomes a "trend" for a month, a week, a day, or sometimes even a couple of hours. When a celebrity makes headlines, when a public company makes a big mistake, when an everyday person goes viral, these "trends" spark a crazy amount of engagement on social media—which you can use to your advantage.

Trend Jacking is where you hop on someone else's train in order to bring some of that heightened attention back to yourself.

This was a very common tactic nearly every top contributing writer used at *Inc Magazine*. We would all set Google Alerts for companies and public figures that aligned with our respective columns, and we'd wait for them to be mentioned in the news. For example, in 2017, Mark Zuckerberg said in an interview that he was changing Facebook's mission. The company's previous mission, "To give people the power to share and make the world more open and connected," was under fire after playing a controversial role in the 2016 presidential election. In this particular interview, Zuckerberg said Facebook was planning to double down on Facebook Groups, and its mission had evolved to, "Giving people the power to build community and bring the world closer together."

Knowing Facebook was all over the news, and knowing *Inc Magazine* wanted to jack the trend, I wrote a piece titled, *Mark Zuckerberg Just Changed Facebook's Mission—Here It Is In 1 Sentence.*

That article became one of my most popular articles ever, accumulating hundreds of thousands of views in a matter of days.

Engagement Hacking

This growth tactic can be very tedious, but it works extremely well.

Engagement Hacking is where you engage with the audiences of other writers, introducing them to your own writing.

The first step is to make a list of other writers *within your chosen category*. If you write about life lessons, go look for other popular writers who also write about life lessons. If you write mystery stories, go find other writers who write mystery stories. Once you have a list of ten or fifteen writers (ideally with audiences similar and slightly larger than your own), go to each of their profiles and start commenting on recent content they've published—or, even better, respond to someone else's comment on their content. For example, if one writer's most recent post was on life lessons you should learn before you turn 30 years old, and someone commented, "I would add a few more to this list," respond back to them and piggy-back on their list to add a few more suggestions of your own.

The whole idea here is to get your name in front of the same people who are actively looking for the type of content you write. When that audience member sees you responded to their comment, they're going to read it. When they read it, and if it's something more thoughtful than just, "Nice one!" they're going to go to your profile.

And when they go to your profile and see that you *actively* write about similar material as the writer they already love and follow, there's a good chance they'll start following you too—especially if they feel like you've started building a relationship with them.

Hashtag Stacking

Most people don't know how hashtags actually work.

A hashtag is nothing more than a folder. It's a way of organizing content that is "tagged" the same thing. When you place a hashtag on a social media post, all you're doing is saying, "This piece of content should be organized in this folder."

The biggest mistake people make when using hashtags is treating them as words and phrases within their actual message. For example, they might post on Facebook: "I just wrote this piece. I hope you enjoy it! #myfirstposteveromg #2020

The hashtag #2020 works, because that's a hashtag a lot of other people use to organize their content. But the hashtag #myfirstposteveromg isn't a folder people are using—and if it is, it's not specific enough to warrant someone using it to search for the content they're trying to find. Which means that hashtag doesn't actually do anything for your distribution efforts.

If you are writing or sharing links to your writing on platforms that use hashtags, the correct way to do hashtag stacking is to do a little research before you post—so you can tag your content with popular, relevant folders. First, go back to your list of popular writers within your chosen category. What hashtags are they using? Why are they using them? For example, one writer might tag all of their posts #writingadvice, because if you're searching for writing advice on a social platform, this is a good folder to start scrolling through. By tagging your posts with that same hashtag, all you're doing is telling the platform to organize this specific post within that folder.

This is step one.

The second step is to then create different tiers of folders for your posts to be organized within. When you click on a hashtag on any social platform, you can see how many people are currently using that hashtag. What you want to do is tag your posts with a blend of both large, popular hashtags and smaller, niche hashtags. For example, #writing is typically a very large folder because it's so broad. A lot of different types of content could be tagged #writing—which means even though you'll be tapping into a wider net of people, you'll also be reaching a more generalized audience. But #businesswriting or #fictionwriting are more specific. They're smaller, in the sense that they're niches and not broad, all-encompassing categories, which means the audiences you'll be tapping into are slightly smaller but potentially more relevant.

The reason I like tagging posts with both broad and niche hashtags is because it gives each post a chance to be exposed to the masses, and to be found by highly targeted readers. We'll talk more about this in the next section, but the entire secret to getting exposure on your writing online is to find as many ways as possible to *make your writing resonate both on a broad level and with a specific audience* at the same time. This is one of those ways.

Publishing Hacking

One of the biggest benefits to building a vast library of content for yourself is the fact that you can continue to leverage that library over and over again.

There are three different components to Publishing Hacking. But in order to understand the best way of doing this, let me clarify the difference between "publishing" and "sharing."

Publishing is the first time you are putting a specific piece of content on one specific platform. Most websites put this in their terms of service, and will eventually flag you for publishing the same content over and over again. For example, on Quora you can't copy/paste the same answer to dozens and dozens of different questions. On Medium, you can't publish the same article more than once. Even on most websites and major publications, you can't have the same article appear in multiple places *unless the publication facilitates this on your behalf* (which is called "syndicating"). So, when in doubt, you'll only want to publish a piece of content once per platform—including on your own website.

Sharing, on the other hand, is the act of taking the link to the original post and recirculating it across various social platforms.

This is what so many companies don't seem to understand about social media marketing, and the incredible return on investment (ROI) that comes with writing online. The bigger you build your library of content, *especially when your content is more timeless than timely,* the more you can continue to engage your audience well into the future.

There's nothing wrong with sharing an article you wrote three years ago—especially if it's a great article.

The three ways you can then leverage your library of content and "hack" the publishing landscape are:

1. **Delete your original post, change a variable or two, and publish it again.**

When you publish something to the internet, there are a million variables that dictate whether or not that piece successfully catches fire.

Maybe you published it during an unlucky time of day. Maybe your original title didn't have the right hook. Maybe you realized after the fact that your post could have been flushed out further. Whatever the reason, there are no rules against deleting your original post and republishing it with a different set of variables. On Quora, this might mean publishing your answer to a different question. On Medium, this might mean changing the headline and adding it to a different publication. On Twitter, this might mean using different hashtags.

The only exception to this rule is if that piece was published on someone else's website or a major publication. Once something goes live in those environments, deleting it becomes a massive hassle and is extremely frowned upon. The reason is because as soon as a piece is live, it's now fair game to be shared and linked to—and what websites and publications want to avoid is a scenario where audience members have already shared or linked to your content, only for your article or story to be taken down and the link to send people to a dead web page.

This same risk also comes with social environments, in the sense that if I write something on Medium and a few people share it on Twitter, then when I choose to delete it, those links are now going to be dead. So the pro/con here is to weigh whether or not the original post accumulated enough attention to warrant "trying again."

My personal advice is to avoid publishing and deleting content as often as possible. Instead, I'm a big believer in just re-writing a new and improved version and publishing a second piece instead. This way, your library continues to expand (opposed to you constantly playing this game of create/delete/create/delete). If you are going to delete a piece, do it within the first 24-48 hours to minimize the number of people who may be sharing it or linking to it.

2. **Build syndication relationships with websites and major publications, and get around the "duplicate content" rule.**

"Syndication" is when major publications build partnerships with each other to share popular content.

For example, I wrote an article in 2016 for *Inc Magazine* titled, *7 Crucial Lessons People Often Learn Too Late In Life*. The article did well on *Inc* and accumulated around 70,000 views. But it wasn't until *Business Insider* syndicated the article that it really caught fire. The first time that article got syndicated, it accumulated more than 3,000,000 views. Six months later, *Business Insider* deleted it (see: above tactic) and republished it again, this time accumulating more than 5,000,000 views. They chose to delete and republish it in order to make this clearly proven content seem as though it was a brand-new article on their site.

This is what I mean when I say that luck plays a major role in how well your content performs. On *Inc*, the article went mini-viral, but because it didn't scratch 100,000 views, I thought it wasn't a winner. Then it got syndicated by *Business Insider* and it went crazy. Which is why it's to your advantage to have your content appear in as many places as possible on the internet. You never know which environment is going to be the one that makes it "go."

However, the "con" of this strategy is what's known as "duplicate content." And since this is the most heavily debated topic in all of content marketing and digital publishing, it's important to understand why I fundamentally disagree with the duplicate content argument—and why I believe syndication is one of the greatest publishing hacks on the internet.

"Duplicate content" is the terminology Google uses to explain their ranking system—and their dislike for seeing the same exact content on multiple websites.

The only time you should be worrying about duplicate content (which means: the same exact content appearing on multiple, different websites) is if you are writing with a heavy focus on SEO—meaning you are running a website and blog, *which is your business*, and you are competing for very specific search terms.

If this is the case, then going back to what I explained at the very beginning of this book, you are not "writing online." You are blogging. For example, let's say you're a life insurance company that wants to rank for the keyphrase "life insurance for seniors." The goal here would be to write a blog post that ranks for that specific keyphrase, so when a potential customer goes to Google and searches "life insurance for seniors," your blog post pops up first.

The reason you wouldn't want this sort of blog post to be syndicated elsewhere is because the entire purpose of writing in this context is to drive sales for the company. You don't really care how many people read this poetic excursion of yours on the benefits of "life insurance for seniors." All you care about is converting potential customers into paying customers. If this is the goal, you're actually going to spend less time writing and publishing new content, and more time getting other websites to backlink to that one individual post, telling Google it is "the best" article on the internet for that particular topic and keyphrase. This is how SEO works.

If you do not fall into this category of bloggers, then you aren't going to be actively optimizing one single post for search. And if you aren't actively optimizing one single post for search, then you gain almost nothing keeping it exclusively on your site—because you are never going to out-compete other blogs (businesses) for the keywords and keyphrases in your article.

In short: writers who fear "duplicate content" think they're doing the right thing, not realizing they're actually playing a completely different game.

Knowing I was never trying to write the #1 ranking blog post for any given keyword or keyphrase, I threw my "duplicate content" fears out the window and went all-in on optimizing for reach. I wanted as many different platforms, with as many different types of audiences, sharing and consuming my content. Whether they read my article on Quora or *Inc Magazine* or my website didn't matter.

What mattered is that they read it, period—and learned who I was as a result.

The beginner version of this strategy is to post every single article you write on every single social platform you can. Every time I write an answer on Quora, for example, I will copy/paste that answer, give it a headline, and also publish it on Medium. Then I'll take that Medium article, copy/paste it, and publish it on LinkedIn. And I'll keep doing this with as many social platforms as I can, where publishing articles of that quality is acceptable. (You can also take this a step further, group articles together, and publish them as eBooks on Wattpad and Amazon, so long as the content is yours.)

Yes, the headlines can be the exact same. No, you don't need to do anything special like change any of the content for SEO purposes—since you aren't playing the SEO game to begin with. All you're doing is sharing your article in different environments, each of which have different ecosystems and audiences.

The advanced version of this strategy is to reach out to websites and publications and let them know you are writing content that aligns with their target audience, and that you'd be willing to let them syndicate your content for free. The reason so many writers don't do this is because, for one, they don't know they can, and two, they have this egoic belief they should be paid by publications for their writing. I have always found this mentality to be incredibly short-sighted. As an up-and-coming writer, I didn't want $100 in exchange for an article. What I wanted was for the publication to open the floodgates and syndicate dozens and dozens of my articles, giving me free marketing, exposure, and Perceived Credibility.

The most effective way to do this is find someone on LinkedIn or Twitter who works for the website or publication, and ideally has "partnerships" somewhere in their job description. Send them a message and say something like:

> *Hey there,*
>
> *My name is Nicolas Cole, and I actively write about personal development habits on Quora and Medium. Since your publication specializes in personal development content, I would love to find a way to collaborate. I'm very passionate about sharing new ideas with people looking to better themselves, and I was wondering if you would be interested in syndicating my content for free.*
>
> *Here are a few of my most popular articles I believe would resonate with your audience:*
>
> - *Link*
> - *Link*
> - *Link*
>
> *Let me know if you'd like to republish any of these! And if this sounds interesting, but these aren't the right fit, just let me know and I'm happy to send you other articles as well.*

Now, most standard websites and conventional blogs probably aren't going to want to syndicate your content—again, because they fear "duplicate content" penalties from Google. But major publications actively syndicate content from social sites such as Quora, Medium, LinkedIn, even Facebook and Twitter, and sometimes have entire departments dedicated to syndicating content onto their sites. They are going to be the most receptive to your outreach—especially if you are writing content that speaks directly to their audience, and you have metrics to prove readership.

This strategy is how I was able to get nearly one hundred articles syndicated from Quora into major publications such as *Forbes, Fortune, TIME, The Chicago Tribune*, etc. And, this strategy is how I have continued to extend my reach as a writer years later. Thrive Global actively syndicates my Medium content. So does The Ladders.

All you have to do is build the partnership yourself.

The expert version of this strategy is the advanced version at the publication level.

This is a publishing growth hack both writers and companies can use, and it's incredibly powerful. Basically, instead of being seen as "a writer" asking publications to syndicate your content, you can build your own website, brand it as a publication, and then forge syndication partnerships with other websites and publications as "a publication" yourself.

The reason this strategy works so well is because the internet is a perception game. If I reach out to *Business Insider* and ask them to syndicate my content, they might say yes—especially if I'm a proven, popular writer online. But a completely different perception is communicated when I say, "Hey there, my name is Cole and I'm heading up the partnerships division of a new life advice publication. I was wondering if you'd be open to syndicating content from our site?" Now, all of a sudden, *Business Insider* isn't chatting with Cole, the writer. They're having a very serious conversation with Cole, the partnerships coordinator, representing an emerging publication.

Obviously there are nuances here. The content you're publishing has to be good enough for the publication to syndicate. The content has to align with their core audience. The content has to both be different enough to be unique, but similar enough to fit within their general style guide. But if these things are all true, a major publication has no reason to decline your free content. No, it won't rank very well on Google, but it's another headline they can share on social media, another page view, and another attempt at "spinning the wheel." And since major publications live and die by website traffic and advertising revenue, the more content, the better.

Once you've created a separate website and publication (which is literally nothing more than a professional-looking Squarespace or Wordpress theme and a bunch of well-written articles from a handful of different authors), you can start plugging your own content into the mix. You can write an answer on Quora. You can copy/paste that answer and publish it as an article on Medium. You can copy/paste that article and publish it again on LinkedIn, and then you can copy/paste that article on LinkedIn onto your brand-new publication, before passing the link along to your point of contact at a major publication, eager to syndicate your content. The best part about this strategy is that you can create as many syndication partnerships as you want. So, in theory, five major publications can all syndicate with your website, and all five can syndicate the exact same article—which can also appear on your social platforms as well.

This is how you quadruple dip in the world of online publishing.

To recap:

- You can publish anything you write in infinite social environments (Quora, Medium, LinkedIn, Wattpad, excerpts on Twitter and Facebook, etc.).

- You can publish articles in infinite social environments and forge partnerships with publications to syndicate your content directly (content originally published on Quora can be syndicated into major publications like *Inc, Forbes, TIME*, etc., IF you facilitate it yourself by reaching out to someone on their syndication/partnerships team).

- You can publish articles in infinite social environments, *and* publish them on a website/publication you own, *and* syndicate them to infinite publications you have partnerships with.

- If you author an article on a major publication first, that article can be republished on your own social profiles (so long as you include a link at the bottom to the original).

- If you author an article on a major publication first, that article can be republished on your own publication (so long as you include a link at the bottom to the original), allowing it to be syndicated to other publications you have partnerships with. Some publications are OK with this, some aren't.

Chapter 6

How To Always Write Something People Will Want To Read: 5 Forms Of Proven Writing

There are five types of writing on the internet.

Form #1: Actionable Guide

Form #2: Opinion

Form #3: Curated List

Form #4: Story

Form #5: Credible Talking Head

Every time you come across an article, a social media post, a free email course, an eBook, etc., I want you to pause and ask the question, "What type of writing is this?" Once you start to see all the different variations these five forms can take on, you will have a greater sense of clarity around what it is you're trying to accomplish every time you sit down to write.

The way you "win" the game of online writing is by creating **the single best possible version** of whatever form of writing you're using **in your chosen category.**

For example, let's say you want to write a How To guide on *how to* become a freelance photographer. The very first question you should ask is, "What type of writing is this?" The answer should be obvious: you're trying to write an "actionable guide." (Tip: "how to" is a dead giveaway you should be using the Actionable Guide form.)

The second question you should ask is, "How can I make this the ULTIMATE guide to writing online?" Your goal should be to create a guide *so specific, so comprehensive, so informative,* that the moment a reader starts reading what you've written, they will immediately 1) bookmark it, 2) share it with someone else, and 3) feel as though they don't need to go read any other guides, articles, or eBooks on the same topic.

Nothing could possibly be "better" than what you've written.

This requires research. It's nearly impossible to know whether or not you've successfully "beaten" the competition if you have no idea who your competition is in the first place. So, poke around the internet. Google the topic you want to write about, along with a handful of related topics. Read a few other people's "ultimate guides," and see if you can pinpoint where they went wrong, or where you (as the reader) wished they had gone more in depth.

Once you've done your due diligence and have a good sense of what you think you need to do to make your piece of writing *the single best resource on the entire internet for that particular topic,* the third question you need to ask yourself is, "Can I make this more specific? Am I trying to cram too much into one article?"

In order to create *the single best resource*, you do not need to write a book. In fact, I have always argued that length is a poor judge of value (the only time this backfired was when a hot-shot restaurateur and potential client said to me, "That's not what my girlfriend thinks," but that's a story for another time). You aren't aiming for a word count. What you're aiming for is the most value you can possibly deliver WITHOUT 1) confusing the reader, or 2) wasting their time.

The usual mistake writers make here is they try to fit too many ideas into one single piece of content. Instead of writing the *single best article* on "How To Land Your First Client As A Freelance Photographer," they write an article that touches a bit on clients, and a bit on lenses, and a bit on accounting, and a bit on photo editing. Even though the title is telling the reader, "I'm about to give you an Actionable Guide," they've unconsciously written a Curated List instead—leaving their reader confused and unfulfilled.

Anytime you fail to deliver on your promise to a reader, **you've lost them.**

Instead, you should write one article exclusively about "How To Land Your First Client As A Freelance Photographer." If any thought, insight, opinion, statistic, story, or random anecdote doesn't have to do with that one specific topic, it shouldn't be in the piece. Period. "How To Choose Your First Lens As A Freelance Photographer" should be a second, separate article. "How To Handle Your Own Accounting As A Freelance Photographer" should be a third, separate article. And so on, ensuring the promise you make to your reader is delivered on to the very best of your ability.

Here's how to do this for all five of the different writing forms.

Actionable Guide

Again, the goal of writing an Actionable Guide of any kind is to get someone to bookmark it.

The reason I like to set this as a "mental goal" is because if you can write something someone is willing to bookmark, that means you've written a resource the reader doesn't want to just read once—but wants to come back to again and again (and not just to that individual piece, but to you as a writer).

There are a handful of ways you can make your Actionable Guide "better" than the competition:

- **"Better" Quality:** If everyone else writes short guides that don't go into very much detail, you can be the one to write long, insightful, walk-through-style guides. Conversely, if everyone else writes long, boring, walkthrough-style guides, you can be the one to condense them into shorter, more digestible bites.

- **"Better" Voice:** If everyone else's How To guides are dense and overwhelming, you can show up to the party and be fast, full of personality, and overly casual. Conversely, if everyone else's How To guides are so casual you feel as though you aren't being given professional insight, you can be the one to write in a more formal way.

- **"Better" Organization:** If everyone else writes really great material, but it's organized poorly and full of huge paragraphs and no subheads or page breaks for the reader, you can win simply by organizing your writing more visually and "appearing" easier to read and understand.

- **"Better" Positioned:** If everyone else is writing about the same problem, you can flip the problem on its head to be seen as something radically different. For example, if there are a million guides all titled "How To Get Your First Client As A Freelance Photographer," you can position yourself differently by reframing the problem: "Freelance Photographers, Here's Why You Don't Want To Charge Your First Client Any Money At All."

- **"Better" For The Audience:** If everyone else is writing about their industry from a broad perspective, you can stand out by choosing not to use universal language and using extremely specific terminology and vernacular only that specific audience would understand—and vice versa, if everyone else writes exclusively for the niche, you can stand out by writing for a broader, more universal audience.

- **"Better" Experience:** If everyone else writes as if they are trying to hard-sell readers into buying a product or course, only giving them 10% of the information they actually need and hoping they'll pay for the other 90%, you can stand out by giving away that same information (and then some) for free.

Opinion

Opinion pieces are, without question, the most popular type of written content on the internet.

Unfortunately, because opinions are so easy to write and share, they are also least likely to stand out because, well, everyone has one. The reason opinions often go unheard is because the people writing them think that "just having an opinion" is the most important measure of success. It's not. Opinions, just like Actionable Guides, have their own set of rules—and if you want to avoid being another navel-gazing blogger nobody cares to listen to, you need to find different ways to communicate in order to stand out.

The techniques listed above for Actionable Guides work well for Opinions, Curated Lists, Stories, and Credibility pieces, so I won't repeat them. Below are additional techniques that work well for Opinion writing.

- **"Better" Data:** If everyone else's opinions are shot from the hip and aren't backed by anything substantial, this is your opportunity to show up to the party with a satchel full of facts. Conversely, if the most popular opinions on a particular topic are overloaded with facts and statistics making them difficult to read, you can be the one to write an entire piece around one single fact and make the topic more digestible.

- **"Better" Quotes:** If everyone else is only writing their own opinions, you can be the one to amplify your opinions by curating credible, insightful quotes from other relevant voices.

- **"Better" Insight:** If everyone else is keeping the conversation within the commonly accepted rules of the industry, you can present insight from outside the industry and expand the conversation to bigger and broader audiences. (And vice versa: if everyone is sharing big, broad opinions, you can be the one to bring the topic back to one key insight.)

- **"Better" Stories:** If everyone else is sharing opinions citing facts or personal beliefs, you can reframe the conversation by telling a unique story that underscores the point you're trying to make. (Writers like Ryan Holiday do this often, where they will tell the reader a story about someone famous or noteworthy from history, and then after telling the story they will expand upon the story with their own personal opinions and insights.)

- **"Better" Clarity:** If everyone else's opinions are murky, disorganized, or unnecessarily complicated, you have an opportunity to make things simple for readers. What really matters here? Why? And how can you say it in a way where a single sentence rings louder than an entire essay on the topic? (For example: Tweets that go massively viral aren't just "clever" or "punchy." They're clear. They resonate with so many people because they bring a massive amount of clarity to an opinion everyone else seems to be overcomplicating.)

Curated List

Ever since the dawn of BuzzFeed, lists on the internet have gotten a bad reputation.

People associate lists with "clickbait." And yes, if the title is "13 Bathing Suits Britney Spears Wore That Reveal The Shape Of Her Nipples," then we're in clickbait territory. But the truth is, a "list" is just another way of organizing information. Who is running for president in the upcoming election is a "list." Which books you should read in order to become a more well-rounded human being is a "list." The greatest basketball players of all time is a "list."

In order for your list to not be clickbait, but actually be meaningful and valuable to a reader, you need two things: Specificity and Speed.

Specificity is how relevant the examples you're choosing in your list are to the target reader. For example, if I'm writing a list of productivity hacks (whether it's an article, or a series of Tweets, or a chapter within an eBook) and half the items on that list aren't really productivity hacks, but time management techniques, well then the reader is going to feel sort of lied to. They were promised "productivity hacks," and I gave them "time management techniques" instead. Or, if I'm writing a list of vampire books you absolutely have to read, but three of the books on the list aren't vampire books but werewolf books, the reader is going to be pissed—and will most likely voice their frustration in the comments.

Speed is then how quickly you are revealing new, important information to the reader. What makes a list "work" is the fact that it has the potential to pack a ton of valuable information into a very short period of time. Again, if I love young adult fiction and I want to know which vampire books I should read this summer, the information I'm interested in (as a reader) is 1) which books, and 2) a quick summary of what each book is about so I can determine which one I want to read first. Anything beyond that is unnecessary, and not why a reader is reading this list in the first place.

Writers go wrong by trying to have one without the other. They optimize for speed, but sacrifice substance—or they optimize for substance, but sacrifice speed.

An example of the former would be, "3 Things You Need To Know About Business," with the three things being 1) You need to work hard, 2) You need to make a profit, and 3) You need to be successful. That list might have speed, but it's essentially worthless to the reader—there isn't enough specificity (in the title, and in the article itself), which means there is very little substance. An example of the latter would be, "3 Things You Need To Know Before Starting Your First Business," with the three things being 1) How to form an LLC, 2) How to do your own accounting, and 3) How to land your first client. Here, the information is more specific and relevant to the target reader, but if it's executed in a long, drawn-out, rambling sort of way, the reader isn't going to read the entire thing.

They're going to look for a "better" version.

In addition to Specificity and Speed, techniques for making your Curated Lists "better" than the competition (in addition to the techniques we've covered above) are:

- **"Better" Examples:** If everyone else is using cliché examples—Michael Jordan, Wayne Gretzky, Tiger Woods—you can differentiate yourself by using lesser known, more unconventional examples specifically from *seemingly irrelevant categories.*

- **"Better" Structure:** If everyone else's lists are numbered subheads followed by big, blocky paragraphs, your lists can appear different just by organizing the information in a cleaner way. Maybe you have a subhead, and then one single sentence of description, before moving on to the next subhead and important piece of information (incredibly fast Rate of Revelation). And vice versa, if everyone else's lists are short and very surface level, there's an opportunity for you to expand upon each numbered point in more depth.

- **"Better" Subheads:** If everyone else is using single-word subheads, why not make your subheads entire sentences? If everyone else is using broad statements as subheads, why not make yours more specific? (This has become a big differentiator for me in my own writing. All of my best-performing lists used this technique where each subhead was a sentence/thought in itself, so that if all a reader did was skim the subheads, they'd get the gist of the entire article.)

- **"Better" Introduction:** If everyone else treats lists as nothing more than a "listing" of information, you have the opportunity to frame your list differently by adding a thoughtful introduction. What makes this list different? Where is this coming from? Who are you to be curating this information for the reader? What's your intention in pulling all this information together? Sharing your point of view as a writer is a powerful mechanism for giving new context to what might be conventional wisdom.

Story

Stories aren't just for fiction writers.

Stories are one of the most powerful ways to "hook" a reader into your piece of writing. The goal of any story should be to move a reader's eyes along the page so quickly that before they can even think to themselves, "Do I want to read this?" they're already off and running.

This was a technique I witnessed very quickly on Quora, and it has become a staple for any high-performing writer on that platform. The answers with the most engagement almost always begin at the absolute height of the story: "The first time I became a millionaire, I was living in my parents' basement." Boom. You're in the story before you've even decided whether or not you wanted to be there in the first place.

Writer and marketer, Josh Fechter, took this strategy and applied it to writing on LinkedIn—and in 2018 actually "broke" LinkedIn's algorithm, accumulating hundreds of millions of views on his long-form status updates. While everyone else was writing short, "Here's what I'm thinking" updates, he started writing short stories about business and entrepreneurship with an insanely high Rate of Revelation. When everyone else was writing and sharing dense paragraphs (as most people do when writing a status update on social media), he gave every single sentence of his short stories its own paragraph. His writing on LinkedIn looked more like a haiku than a status update.

All these little choices he made were ways his writing became "better" than everyone else's—and he beat the game as a result.

Techniques for making your Stories "better" than the competition (in addition to all the other techniques described above) are:

- **"Better" Openers:** If everyone else is taking their sweet time getting to the point, blow right past them and start writing at the moment of conflict or achievement. (Every single sentence you write online, you are fighting for the reader's attention. If your story "gets better" four paragraphs later, delete your first four paragraphs. You don't need them.)

- **"Better" Transitions:** If everyone else is writing long-winded, overly descriptive, and slow-as-molasses prose, do the opposite. Tell an entire story in four sentences. Add a page break. And then move on to the next powerful story or thought. There are no rules in writing. All that matters is you keep the reader's eyes moving down the page.

- **"Better" Characters:** If everyone else in your niche or genre names their characters regular names like John and Sarah, name your characters XY-2 and UU-5. If everyone else's characters have regular hobbies like playing soccer or the guitar, give your characters more unique hobbies like tie-dying safari hats. Whether you're creating fictional characters in your imagination, or choosing true stories to retell, you always want to be searching for the unconventional. Remember: what's expected is boring. What's *unexpected* is exciting, new, and different.

- **"Better" Language:** If everyone else is writing in formal English with perfect grammar, try writing in a dialect only your most loyal readers will understand. Maybe you intentionally never use commas because that's your style. Maybe you intentionally overuse the word 'like' because, like, you want to sound like a valley girl because like, that would just be just like so perfect for your story. (The book *Clockwork Orange* is a terrific example of how language can be manipulated to create a cult following and a very special relationship with your readers.)

- **"Better" Category:** If everyone else is writing conventional sci-fi, you should be the one to write Education Sci-Fi, where you teach readers different subject matters but in futuristic terms, settings, etc. Or, if everyone else is writing cooking recipes with a few personal anecdotes, you should be the one to write Recipes That Became Family Stories— giving the reader a recipe they can make themselves, but also telling them *the ridiculous time Uncle Larry tried to make apple pie and ended up at the grocery store at 1:00 a.m., hammered, arguing with the cashier lady about how NASA has never actually been to the moon and they staged the whole thing on live television*. Writing that truly "stands out" always lives in a fundamentally different category.

Credible Talking Head

And finally, there are things on the internet that get read simply because they're "the most credible."

When a news story breaks, people want to know what the *New York Times* has to say about it. When the NBA announces they're going to change a rule, the world wants to know how Michael Jordan, Larry Bird, Shaquille O'Neal, and other former professional basketball players feel about "how the game has changed." When a new pharmaceutical drug hits the market, readers want to know what doctors have to say about it. And when you want to know how to start writing online, the first question you ask yourself is, "Who should I turn to for advice? Who is the most *credible*?"

Your goal as a writer is to always be looking for the topics, subject matters, and categories you are most qualified to write within.

"Write what you know," as the adage goes.

Sometimes, your credibility informs what it is you write about (you're the Head of Marketing for a startup, and so you believe you're qualified to write about marketing). Other times, what you write about informs how and where you need to build your credibility. For example, I started writing about personal development on Quora when I was 24 years old. I wasn't some highly qualified life coach or esteemed motivational speaker giving advice. I didn't have any credibility at all. But the more I wrote, and the more people read my writing, and the more publications republished my work, the more I "grew into" my credibility.

Techniques for making any of your writing that leans on Credibility "better" than the competition (in addition to all the other techniques described above) are:

- **"Better" Association:** If everyone else is writing only about their own personal experiences, write about your personal experiences being surrounded by or spending time with Barack Obama, Bill Gates, Brad Pitt, Halle Berry, or whoever else is seen as credible *in your chosen category*. (Name-dropping is one of the fastest ways to tell a reader, "I know what I'm talking about.")

- **"Better" Context:** If everyone else is giving advice or sharing their opinions, you should be the one to give context as to why your advice, opinion, or story is different. For example, it's one thing for me to say, "There are 5 things you need to know about ghostwriting for executives." But, it's much more powerful if I say, "I learned a lot building a multi-million-dollar ghostwriting company, and let me tell you, there are 5 things you need to know about ghostwriting for executives." That one small addition of credibility completely changes the context of everything that follows.

- **"Better" Arguments:** If everyone else is just stating the facts, or shooting opinions from the hip, you can be the one to challenge conventional wisdom. Instead of writing about what to do, write about what *not* to do. Instead of talking about things people should learn, talk about what things most people *never* learn—and fail as a result. Reframing a topic is a powerful way of communicating to readers that you know something most other people *in your chosen category* do not.

- **"Better" Perception:** If everyone else's eBook covers look like all the other eBooks *in your chosen category,* go seek out a designer who has a polar-opposite style so that your eBook looks nothing like the competition. If everyone else's photos on social media look cheap and amateurish, save up some money and invest in professional photos, making yourself look like you've got a massive publishing house behind you (even if you don't). The more ways you can present yourself as "unlike the rest," the better.

Chapter 7

The Perfect Post: How To Write Headlines People Can't Help But Read

Every form of online writing has a headline.

The first sentence of your Facebook post or Tweet is "a headline."

The title and subtitle of your Wattpad or Amazon eBook is "a headline."

The front page of your company website is "a headline."

Why people read certain things on the internet and not others is often a reflection of its headline. That string of five to fifteen words at the very top of the page tells the reader whether the piece of writing in front of them is going to be worth their time—and what they can expect in exchange for reading it.

What makes a great headline is getting someone to understand three things at the exact same time:

1. What this piece of writing is about

2. Who this piece of writing is for

3. The PROMISE: the problem that will be solved, and/or the solution being offered

This is what's known as The Curiosity Gap.

The Curiosity Gap is what tells the reader what this piece of writing is about, who it's for, and what it's promising— all without revealing the answer.

When it comes to headlines, writers will often aim to write something "creative" or "clever," failing to realize that true creativity is actually the art of *clarity*. If you're vague, people won't know what it is you're writing about. If you're unspecific, they won't know it's for them. And if your PROMISE isn't compelling enough, they won't give it any attention.

For example, a headline like "The Big Idea" is ineffective because it doesn't tell the reader 1) what it's about, 2) who it's for, or 3) what it's promising in exchange.

Here's how we fix it:

- **"The Big Idea That Needs To Get Through Politicians' Heads To Fix Racial Inequality In America"** is clearer. As a reader, you now know exactly what this piece is about.

- **"3 Big Ideas From Steve Jobs, Elon Musk, And Jeff Bezos That Changed The World Forever"** is more specific. If you're interested in creativity and business, you know this article was written for you.

- **"This 1 Big Idea Will Change The Way You Think About College"** is a big PROMISE. This headline tells the reader, "The way you think about college will no longer be the same after you read this article."

And you better deliver on that PROMISE—otherwise readers are going to call your writing "clickbait."

*(People think "clickbait" refers to the headline style that uses numbers: 7 Things, 6 Ways, 3 Mistakes, etc. It's not. These headline styles are extremely effective **as long as you keep your PROMISE to the reader.** It's when you don't keep your PROMISE that the reader feels tricked—which leaves them disappointed, angry, and "click-baited.")*

Now, there are definitely some lazy, overly sensational examples of The Curiosity Gap that writers on the internet use all the time, and I don't recommend them.

- "You'll Never Believe What Happened Next!"

- "This CRAZY Situation Couldn't Have Gotten ANY WORSE"

- "The Secret No One Wants You To Know..."

"Better," less clickbaity examples of The Curiosity Gap would be headlines that more articulately speak to the intended audience, problem, and PROMISE.

- "The 1 Mistake All New Project Managers Make—That Ends Up Costing Their Company $500,000"

- "7 Small But Meaningful Things You Can Say To Your Significant Other To Show How Much You Love Them"

- "How To Write Headlines That Go Viral, Accumulate Millions Of Page Views, And Convert Readers Into Loyal Customers"

What makes these headlines so powerful isn't that they're "creative" or "clever." They're powerful because they are *clear* in their intentions. You know exactly what each one of these pieces is going to be about before you even click on it—which means, if a reader does choose to click on an article, they didn't arrive there on accident. Something about the headline spoke to them (and the more you write, and the more data you accumulate, you will begin to know which types of headlines speak to your target readers most effectively).

Expert-level examples of The Curiosity Gap are headlines that find new, unique ways to achieve these same three goals but by using new language, structures, or formats. Best-selling books do this masterfully. They combine an overarching main title with an ultra-specific subtitle to create a puzzle of intrigue.

Nonfiction Examples

- "Atomic Habits: An Easy & Proven Way To Build Good Habits & Break Bad Ones"

- "The 4-Hour Workweek: Escape 9-5, Live Anywhere, And Join The New Rich"

- "Play Bigger: How Pirates, Dreamers, And Innovators Create And Dominate Markets"

Fiction Examples

- "The Book Thief" (Look at how much you can imagine about the story based off just those three words!)

- "Ready Player One" (Immediately tells gamers, "This is a book for you.")

- "The Martian" (When paired with a photo of a human on Mars, the reader immediately knows "The Martian" isn't some otherworldly creature inhabiting earth—it's actually about a human inhabiting another planet.)

What these titles have in common is they are executing The Curiosity Gap with two puzzle pieces instead of just one. On the nonfiction side, "Escape 9-5, Live Anywhere, And Join The New Rich" is a great headline. But it's a "better" headline by adding "The 4-Hour Workweek" in front of it. There's a clearer benefit, another PROMISE. And on the fiction side, the entire story arc is told in two or three carefully chosen words. It's not just that the title is "catchy." The reason these titles work is because the reader actually gets all three of their questions answered clearly:

1. What is this about?

2. Is this for me?

3. What PROMISE are you making—and how confident am I in your ability to deliver on that PROMISE?

Who Are You Writing For?

Before you start writing *anything*, the very first thing you should do is think deeply about the headline, the frame, and the focal point you are presenting to your reader.

Even if you're writing a 100-character Tweet, I encourage you to question, "What would be the headline of this Tweet?"

To be honest, I used to write my headlines last. A younger me believed what mattered more was the content of what I was saying, and that the headline was basically just the bow I placed on top. Seven years later, I realized this was not only incorrect, but incredibly unproductive. Your headline isn't just a headline. Your headline is, quite literally, a micro-version of your entire Actionable Guide, Opinion, Curated List, Story, or Credible Talking Head monologue.

If you can't clearly communicate what it is you want to say in a twelve-word headline, chances are, you won't clearly communicate what it is you want to say in an 800-word post (or a 60,000-word book).

The first question I encourage you to ask yourself is, "Who is this piece of writing for?"

One of the biggest ironies when it comes to online writing is that people think Audience and Subject Matter are two completely separate variables. They sit down to write whatever it is they want to write, and then, *after the fact*, they say, "Ok now how do I get this in front of a billion people?"

What these writers fail to realize is that Subject Matter is actually what *defines* the size of their Audience.

**The size of your audience is a direct reflection of the
size of the question you're answering.**

For example, very few people wake up in the morning
and say to themselves, "Wow, I wonder what's new in the
world of biotechnology." Biotechnology is a niche. Which
means, if you're writing about what's happening within the
world of biotechnology, your Audience will only be as big
as the number of people actively asking themselves about
biotechnology.

However, a lot more people wake up in the morning and
ask themselves, "How can I be happier in life? How do
I know if I'm in a healthy relationship? How can I make
more money?"

These broader, more universal questions have much
larger Audiences—which means, by choosing Happiness,
Relationships, or Money as your Subject Matter, you will
inherently reach a wider Audience.

Before you begin writing anything, you need to decide
who you are writing for. And that decision needs to be
clearly reflected in both the headline and the content of
your piece.

Are you writing for the masses? Do you want to try
to reach as many people as possible? Then you need to
answer a universal question—something that will resonate with anyone, no matter who they are or where
they're from.

Are you writing for a specific niche? Are you less
concerned with reaching "everyone," and more concerned
with reaching a specific type of person? Then you need to

answer a question highly relevant to that niche—
something that will resonate meaningfully with your exact
target reader (for example: someone deep in the field of
biotechnology).

This is true for both fiction and nonfiction. A story
titled, "The Day Humans Went Extinct" answers a much
broader question ("What happens if every human goes
extinct?") than a story titled, "The Day Vampires Went
Extinct." Why? Because the number of people who want to
know about the future of *humans* is much larger than the
number of people who want to know about the future of
vampires. And even less people want to read a story titled,
"The Day Caterpillar-Vampires Went Extinct." As the size of
the question gets smaller, and the niche gets more specific,
so does the size of your potential Audience.

**Now, there is a way for you to get the best of both
worlds, and that's by using niche topics to answer universal questions.**

For example, an article titled, "How To Be A Better Writer"
answers two of our three questions. You know who this
article is going to be for, and you know what it's going
to be about. Unfortunately, the PROMISE is a little weak.
What does being a "better writer" really mean? What
benefits do you receive by becoming a better writer? Why
should someone want to become a "better writer" in the
first place?

Here is where you have a decision to make. You can either
make your PROMISE answer a niche question or a broad
question—and depending on which you pick will dramatically change the size of your potential Audience. (It will
also change the content of the piece.)

For example:

"How To Be A Better Writer Today, So You Can Start Writing Best-Selling Books Tomorrow" would be a title with a big PROMISE for aspiring authors. If you have no interest in becoming a best-selling author, you probably won't want to read this piece of writing. It's more specific, and will resonate more clearly with your target reader, but it won't reach as many different types of readers. This is the pro/con.

"How To Become A Better Writer, Journal More Often, And Live A More Present Life," on the other hand, has a completely different PROMISE. The question it's answering is dramatically bigger ("How can I live a more present life?"). The Curiosity Gap here is saying that by *becoming a better writer*, and using writing as a habit, you can live a more present life.

This technique of tying niche topics to universal questions is a powerful way of tapping into new audiences and expanding your reach outside of your particular industry or category.

Here are a few more examples:

- "The Future Of The Biotechnology Industry" is niche (and vague), and can be expanded by changing it to "How The Future Of Biotechnology Is Going To Make All Of Us Happier, Healthier, And Live Longer."

- "The Girl Who Ran Away" is good, but it can be clarified and expanded by changing it to, "The Girl Who Ran Away: Family, Loss, And The

Power Of Forgiving Those Who Hurt You Most."

- "7 Tips For Becoming Smarter" is clear, but a bigger PROMISE can help it reach more people. "7 Tips For Becoming Smarter, Achieving Chess-Master Memory, And Becoming The Most Interesting Person In The Room"

To recap:

- Bigger Questions attract Bigger Audiences

- Niche Questions attract Niche Audiences

- Wider Audiences benefit from simple, universal language

- Niche Audiences benefit from ultra-specific, niche language

- Titles that only answer 1 of the 3 questions are weak. Titles that answer 2 of the 3 questions are good. Titles that answer all 3 of the questions are exceptional

Pieces Of A Perfect Headline

The 1 Question *That Gets* *Every Single Millennial* {In Trouble}

This is a headline from an article I wrote for *Inc Magazine* that ended up accumulating over 200,000 views. It ended up attracting a lot of attention from other publications, smaller blogs, and even podcasters, all of whom wanted to have a debate about Millennials in the workforce.

To clearly explain what makes a headline great, we need to examine each of the pieces within a headline by itself—so you can see how they fit into the whole. I've coded the above headline with different symbols (bold, underline, **, italics, and {}), so we can get into the weeds here and talk about each piece of the sentence.

The 1:

The first two or three words of a headline are arguably the most important words of the sentence. When people are scrolling through titles, they really only look at the beginning and the end. They want to know what this "thing" is (the beginning), and what will happen (the end/the PROMISE) if they read it—all in a matter of milliseconds.

The beginning of this headline here immediately sets the tone: **The 1.**

That's it.

There's 1 and 1 only.

There are two reasons this technique of using a number at the beginning of a headline is so effective. First, it conveys conviction, which readers trust. It's declarative, and anything that is declarative implies a strong stance or opinion (which people love). Second, it sounds short. You're not asking the reader to read about 10 different points, or 100 different points. You're saying, "You just need to know this 1 thing," which feels like a very low barrier to entry for a reader.

"Meh, this will only take me a second to read," they say to themselves, right before they click.

Question

Next, **The 1** has to describe something. The 1... <u>what</u>?

- Reason?
- Way?
- Solution?
- Problem?

This part of the sentence is <u>the what</u>. It's the carrot you dangle in front of the reader letting them know <u>what</u> they're about to read. Without this in the sentence, every reader will subconsciously feel like the headline lacks clarity—and when you confuse, you lose.

The real key to choosing the right word for this part of the headline is to think about what will stir up the most curiosity in your audience.

This is the beginning of your Curiosity Gap.

That Gets

This is the part of the headline that connects the beginning to the end.

Connecting pieces should be used sparingly. Nobody has time for a 20-word headline, and every additional word you add is one more step the reader needs to slog through in order to figure out what the headline is saying, who it's for, and what they can expect to receive in exchange for reading it.

Now, based on your genre, category, or topic, you might not even need these connecting pieces. If you do, make sure to pick strong, descriptive words. For example, "Gets" is a conversational word, which works well for broader audiences, but truthfully (and this would mean shifting other words in the sentence), "Incentivizes" or "Pushes" or "Encourages" would be better words. They're more descriptive.

Every Single Millennial

This is the WHO.

WHO is this article for? Entrepreneurs? Artists? Millennials? Baby Boomers? And more importantly, within that demographic, WHO specifically? All of them? Some of them? One specific group of them?

This is the part of the sentence that caters most to your target audience. Your WHO doesn't have to be an age demographic. It could be a group of people joined together by an interest or even a place. In a title like "4 Things All Chicagoans Need To Do…," the WHO is "Chicagoans," which also implies a WHERE as well.

The two things you need to balance here are:

- WHO—based on age, ethnicity, location, interest, etc.

- WHO within that WHO—all of them? Some of them? 1% of them?

{In Trouble}

And finally, the ending—also known as THE PROMISE.

This is what readers look for most. They want to know what happens in the story before they even read it.

The key to writing a great PROMISE is to use language that elicits an emotional response. "Trouble" is a great word because nobody likes getting into trouble, yet everyone loves hearing about other people who get in trouble.

The best way to come up with a compelling PROMISE is to think deeply about 1) outcomes your readers want to receive, or 2) outcomes your readers want to avoid.

For example:

- "...Become Rich" is a good outcome, but "...Become So Rich You Never Have To Think About Money Again" is a far more emotional and exciting outcome.

- "...Not Lose Your Job" is a general outcome most people want to avoid, but "...Not Get Fired On Your First Day" is a more specific, more easily imaginable outcome a lot of people actively worry about.

- "...Get Married" is a standard outcome, but "...Get Married And Stay Together For More Than 20 Years" is an outcome the reader can measure.

The more emotional you can make your PROMISE, the more likely a reader is to want to read, comment, and share your writing.

Because it speaks to a part of their identity.

Proven Headline Formats

Once you know how a headline is constructed, you can then start adding and subtracting different puzzle pieces to hook your target reader's attention.

There are a handful of headline formats that writers, major publications, and publishing houses use relentlessly—because they work. It's the reason why nearly every *Business Insider* or *Forbes* article has a similar look and feel, and why each genre has its patterns. My recommendation for using these proven formats is to think of ways you can incorporate them into your individual style.

Here are some of the most proven headline formats in online writing:

- **Big Numbers:** For example, "3,000 People Just Filed For Unemployment In This Small Town In Arkansas. Here's Why." This is a great headline because "3,000 People" is concrete, definitive, easy to imagine, and yet an unexpectedly large number—and what's unexpected is exciting.

- **Dollar Signs:** Money is about as universal as a topic can get. "$400 Million Is How Much You Need To Make In Order To Afford This Insane Mansion In Malibu" is eye-catching because very few people have $400 million. Dollar signs make the Curiosity Gap wider and more interesting for readers.

- **Credible Names:** Celebrities, CEOs, pop culture icons, anyone the world can easily recognize by name is a great way to hook readers' attention. "Will Smith's Advice On How To Live A Fulfilling Life Will Change The Way You See The World Forever" is a headline built on credibility. Yes, there's a great PROMISE here, but the real "hook" comes from the fact that it's advice from Will Smith. "Amazon, Apple, Tesla, And 4 Other Stocks That Have Made Early Investors Mega-Millionaires" is another example of how to leverage name credibility.

- **"This Just Happened":** Timeliness is a terrific mechanism for getting readers' attention *right now*. Words like "Just, Recently, Today, Now," etc., are what tell a reader that of all the things on the internet to read, "this thing" is high priority. For example, "Michael Jordan Just Gave A Press Conference And NBA Executives Are Furious." The reason you would want to read that article is to feel in-the-know.

- **The Success Story:** These headlines summarize an amazing event or rare occurrence that doesn't happen every day. For example, "How This Small Team Managed To Secure A Six-Figure Investment In Less Than 1 Week" or "This 1 Group Activity Exercise Increased An Entire Office's Productivity By 150%."

- **Things That Shouldn't Go Together:** Combining two or more things in a headline that don't typically sit next to each other is a great way to force readers to pause and take an interest. For example, "7 Things KFC And Miley Cyrus Have In Common," or, "What Jay-Z, Pablo Escobar, And Oprah Can Teach Us About Leadership."

- **For The Industry:** These headlines work well when you're writing for a very specific audience. So much so, that you want to call them out right in the title. The more specific you can be about who the piece is for, the better. For example, "3 Things All Successful Small Business Owners Do To Stay Profitable."

- **The Topic Within The Topic:** Some headlines benefit from a bit of added curiosity. This is a technique that can be applied to any of the other headline structures, and can be a great way of making readers feel like they're getting the "inside scoop." For example, "7 Ways The Real Estate Industry Is Changing (And How You Should Be Investing Your Money)." The first part of the headline is strong, but it's the second part of the headline (inside parentheses) that gives the first part more context.

- **Question/Answer:** These headlines start with a question and end with a hint at the answer. This style is best suited for articles with a big concept that's difficult to cram into one headline—but when split in two, you're able to give more context to the reader, faster. For example, "Can't Be Productive In The Office? Try Organizing Your Calendar Like This" or "Don't Know How To Track Your Goals? This New App Has The Answer."

- **X Number:** 1 Thing, 3 Ways, 5 Lessons, 9 Habits, etc. Placing a number at the beginning of a headline tells the reader, "This is all you're signing up for—just 9 quick habits and then we're done." It makes the piece feel like there is a much lower barrier to entry, while at the same time setting a concrete expectation. The book, "13 Things Mentally Strong People Don't Do" became an international bestseller using the same headline style that has powered so many articles online.

And of course, you can combine any of these proven formats to make your headlines even stronger. For example, "The 1 Thing LeBron James Does Every Morning That Earns Him An Extra $10 Million Per Year."

BuzzFeed has a rule: **every writer must write 30 versions of a headline** in order to find the right one.

All great headlines take time.

The first headline you write probably won't be "it." There's a rewriting process that needs to happen in order to get rid of all the tiny words like "if, when, does, it, too, for," etc., that get in the way of your headline achieving all three of its goals: 1) telling the reader what this piece is about,

2) whether it's for them, and 3) whether the PROMISE is worth their time.

The way I write and rewrite headlines is I first try to say whatever it is I'm trying to say, in as many words as I need to say it.

"The 8 Things You Should Do On A Daily Basis In Order To Become The Best Person You Can Possibly Become, No Matter What Obstacles Are In Your Way"

Next, I think hard about whether or not I've really nailed down the PROMISE. Can I PROMISE more? What else does the reader want? What are their emotional wants, needs, and desires related to this specific problem or piece of advice?

"The 8 Things You Should Do On A Daily Basis In Order To Get More Done, Achieve Your Goals, And Start Living Your Best Life"

Then, once I feel like I have clarity around the PROMISE, I look for words that are still too vague. I want the reader's eyes to skim my headline and latch on to two or three words that speak directly to the categories of their interests.

*"The 8 Things You Should Do On A Daily Basis To Be More **Productive**, Achieve **Success**, And Gain **True Financial Freedom**"*

Finally, I'll go through my headline and edit out as many tiny connecting words as possible. Less is more.

"8 Daily Habits That Will Make You More Productive, Achieve Success, And Gain True Financial Freedom"

If I get to the end of the exercise and I like the headline in its final form, I'll go and write the piece. And if I went through the steps and felt like I didn't end up with something powerful enough, I'll start back at the beginning.

If you are a nonfiction writer, then I strongly encourage you to use these techniques in your online writing. Once you learn the formats, you'll start to see them everywhere—from Medium articles to *New York Times* headlines. Again, I'm not advocating for you to sound like you're a *BuzzFeed* columnist. All I'm doing is pointing out the techniques that work, so you can best decide how to mold them to match your own unique style.

And if you are a fiction writer, then I would encourage you to apply these techniques to your story titles, as well as your content marketing. If you want to write a sci-fi book, you should also be writing articles online like, "8 Timeless Sci-Fi Characters That Defined The Genre Forever." Because chances are, if someone is interested in reading an article like that, they're also interested in new sci-fi stories like your own—which you can subtly mention at the beginning or end of the piece.

POWER Phrases

Lastly, you always want to be thinking about what "POWER phrases" you can add to your headlines to clarify the urgency and importance of whatever it is you're writing about.

For example, instead of saying "7 Ways…" you could say, "7 Little-Known Ways" or "7 Small But Powerful Ways." These tiny tweaks are what tell readers that what they're about to read is *different* from all the other articles on the same topic—and can also hint at a more meaningful or impactful PROMISE.

A few examples:

- 3 **Crucial** Lessons About Business You'll Learn Working For A High-Growth Startup Founder

- These **Unforgettable** Tips From Silicon Valley's 10 Most Successful VC Firms Will Change The Way You Think About Business Forever

- 9 **Memorable** Truths About Life They Don't Teach You In School

- This 1 **Eye-Opening** Takeaway From The 2019 TED Conference Will Inspire You To Be The Next Success Story In Your Industry

- 11 **Painful** Mistakes Most Founders Make Right After Raising Their First Round Of Fundraising

- 4 **Emerging** Biotech Trends You Should Know Are Quietly Changing The World

Chapter 8

The Art Of Writing Online: How To Structure The Perfect Post

There is no "one" correct way to write online.

Every day, new writers emerge on the internet that redefine the rules of the game. That's what makes the game fun, and what keeps creators on their toes.

However, there are absolutely techniques the most popular writers use in order to cater to the consumption habits of today's readers. We forget that art is always a reflection of society, and writers today are competing in a world where attention is in short supply. As a result, the writing styles that thrive in today's environment are ones that move quickly, and respect the reader's time as much as humanly possible.

If you can say it in three sentences instead of five, try to say it in two.

And if you can say it in two sentences, do your very best to say it in one.

Viral articles, Twitter threads, and any other effective piece of written content online follows this basic structure:

Section 1: Introduction

Section 2: X Main Points

Section 3: Conclusion

As soon as a reader clicks on your headline and says to themselves, "Sure, I'll bite," your writing is now racing against their dwindling attention span. A reader will only continue reading as long as they have a reason to—and every second that passes is another moment for them to question, "Why am I still here? Is this worth my time?"

So, here's how you hook them—and keep them hooked until the end of your piece.

As we dig into examples here, I encourage you to skim this chapter and return to it as needed. I'll be getting very in-the-weeds, so please don't feel the need to make your way through each example linearly.

The Art Of Writing Introductions

Right away in the introduction, your job is to answer all three of the reader's preliminary questions:

1. What is this about?

2. Is this for me?

3. What are you PROMISING and how confident am I that you're going to deliver on that PROMISE?

The very first sentence is arguably the most important sentence of the entire piece.

It should be a short sentence. It should be a clear sentence. It should be a sentence that a reader can fly through, giving them the feeling they're off to a running start. You are successful if you can nail the entire "point" of the piece in ten words or less.

- "Most people don't believe me when I say I write 10,000 words per day, every day." This is the first sentence of my viral article, "How I Write 10,000 Words Per Day, Every Day."

- "Success doesn't happen in an instant." This is the first sentence of my viral article, "19 Tiny Habits That Lead To Huge Results."

- "There are only 2 ways to become rich." This is the first sentence of my viral article, "The 1 Habit That Keeps 99% Of People From Ever Becoming Rich."

Once this sentence has answered the reader's first question ("What is this about?"), you now have a very limited amount of time to answer their second and third questions—"Is this for me, and what are you PROMISING?"

There are a handful of rhythms you can use to answer the remaining two questions and craft an effective introduction.

1/3/1

The 1/3/1 structure is the best place to start.

In 1/3/1, you have one strong opening sentence, three description sentences, and then one conclusion sentence. Visually, this is a powerful way to tell the reader you aren't going to make them suffer through big blocks of text, and that you have their best interests in mind.

Here's how it works:

This first sentence is your opener.

This second sentence clarifies your opener. This third sentence reinforces the point you're making with some sort of credibility or amplified description. And this fourth sentence rounds out your argument, guiding the reader toward your conclusion.

This fifth sentence is your strong conclusion.

Now, just so you can understand why this technique is so powerful, not just from a written perspective but from a visual perspective, look at those same five sentences all clumped together.

This first sentence is your opener. This second sentence clarifies your opener. This third sentence reinforces the point you're making with some sort of credibility or amplified description. And this fourth sentence rounds out your argument, guiding the reader toward your conclusion. This fifth sentence is your strong conclusion.

If you clicked on an article and were immediately confronted with a five-sentence paragraph, you would feel (viscerally in your body) the weight of what you were about to read.

That feeling of weight is what you are always trying to lift off your readers' shoulders.

Easy reading makes them feel light.

Here's an example of the 1/3/1 structure from my article, "How Do Some People Succeed So Quickly? They Approach Life Like This."

> *Life is all about perspective.*
>
> *The exact same situation can be perceived in very different ways by two different people. One might see loss — the other, opportunity. One might feel like a victim — the other, a change-maker. Which means, as far as "absolute" truths are concerned, the first step to becoming who you truly want to be in life means accepting the fact that how you see the world might not be the whole picture.*
>
> *So, if our life experience is based upon the way we see the world, then here are some small but incredibly impactful mental shifts that can help you see things from a new perspective.*

The last sentence of the 1/3/1 article should be both a conclusion and a transition into the next section of the article—your Main Points. This way, the reader feels as though they've reached their first "checkpoint" reading your piece (giving them a feeling of accomplishment) while also hinting at where you are going to take them next.

This is what keeps them emotionally connected and invested in reading more.

1/5/1

The 1/5/1 structure is the same as the 1/3/1 structure, just with more room for description and clarification in the middle.

Here's how it works:

> *This first sentence is your opener.*
>
> *This second sentence clarifies your opener. This third sentence reinforces the point you're making with some sort of credibility or amplified description. This fourth sentence builds on that credibility or description, giving added context or new information. This fifth sentence explains to the reader why you're telling them what you're telling them. And this sixth sentence drives home the point.*
>
> *This seventh sentence is your strong conclusion.*

You want to use the 1/5/1 structure when your opener would benefit from additional context, or you want to tell a story that requires an extra sentence or two for clarification. However, once you start getting into 1/7/1 or 1/8/1 territory, you're either trying to tackle too many different points at once, or you are being unnecessarily descriptive. There are cases where having this big of a middle paragraph can work, but I would encourage you to stay away from it—and if you do, then your opener sentence and your conclusion sentence should be very short (to counterbalance the big block of text between them).

Here's an example of the 1/5/1 structure, from my *Inc Magazine* article, "Being A Freelancer Is Not The Same As Being An Entrepreneur. Here's Why."

The dream before you take the leap to become a full-time entrepreneur is to have "work-life balance."

I remember back when I was working my 9-5, a little over a year ago. I had to commute an hour to work each way, which made my commitment closer to an 8-6. And then some days I would need to work late, which meant I wouldn't leave until 7, or sometimes 8. I'd finally make it home, throw my backpack onto my bed, and sit in my desk chair with the sullen realization that the day was over. I had enough time to cook dinner and do a little late-night writing before passing out and repeating the same dance all over again.

Becoming an entrepreneur, I thought, would give me more time to enjoy some of my other passions.

Again, the purpose of organizing your introductions using a structure like this is to both verbally and visually tell readers what "type" of writing they're about to read.

A 1/3/1 or 1/5/1 opener = easy to read.

A 7-sentence opening paragraph = difficult to read.

1/3/2/1 & 1/5/2/1

The basic structures of online writing are 1/3/1 and 1/5/1.

Once you learn these, you can then start to play with rhythm a bit more and elongate your introductions.
I cannot stress enough how much you *do not want* to

elongate your writing by cramming sentence after sentence into one paragraph. Online writing benefits from clearly separated thoughts and statements, which is why I recommend using variations of the 1/3/1 and 1/5/1 structure if you need the extra space.

Remember: you want to optimize for speed and Rate of Revelation.

Anything that isn't absolutely necessary, delete it.

Here's how it works:

> *This first sentence is your opener.*
>
> *This second sentence clarifies your opener.*
> *This third sentence reinforces the point you're making with some sort of credibility or amplified description. And this fourth sentence rounds out your argument, guiding the reader toward your conclusion.*
>
> *This fifth sentence is your strong conclusion. And this sixth sentence is expanding on why you're making such a strong conclusion.*
>
> *This seventh sentence is what you're going to talk about next.*

Here, the 1/3/1 structure is being expanded ever so slightly into 1/3/2/1, without asking the reader to slog through too much additional description or explanation. And with the 1/5/2/1 structure, you're doing the same thing just expanding it a tiny bit more. Notice, we are still keeping one single sentence as the opener, and one single sentence as the conclusion. This is to visually tell the reader, "You already read the first sentence, now there's just this one big paragraph and then you can already see the conclusion sentence waiting for you."

When readers can "see" the end, they're more likely to want to put in the effort to get there.

1/4/1/1

Why the 1/4/1/1 structure works so well is because now your single-sentence conclusion packs two punches instead of one.

Here's how it works:

> *This first sentence is your opener.*
>
> *This second sentence clarifies your opener. This third sentence reinforces the point you're making with some sort of credibility or amplified description. This fourth sentence rounds out your argument. And this fifth sentence speaks to the emotional benefit of the reader.*
>
> *This sixth sentence is your conclusion.*
>
> *And this seventh sentence is why that conclusion matters so much.*

If you notice, the only difference between the 1/3/1 structure and 1/4/1/1 is rhythm.

One more sentence doesn't really change the content of the introduction. But the way the sentences are separated elicits a different response in the reader. The 1/3/1 structure feels strong, but 1/4/1/1 feels stronger, and even more opinionated—there are two punchlines instead of one. In fact, just by moving a single sentence up or down in any of these paragraphs can dramatically change the rhythm of your introduction.

Here's an example of the 1/4/1/1 structure from my article, "6 Important Life Lessons You Can Only Learn Through Failure."

> *Nobody learns the hard lessons in life without some element of failure.*
>
> *When we let someone down, we learn why. When we fall short of our own expectations, we become aware of our growth edge. When we crumble under pressure, we become attuned to our weaknesses. There is a "lesson" inside each and every defeat — and those who ultimately reach their goals see these moments as valuable opportunities, not punishments.*
>
> *Unfortunately, that doesn't make the learning process any less painful.*
>
> *There are some lessons in life you just can't learn without falling down, scraping both knees, and getting back up again.*

Like the other structures above, you can elongate your introduction by adding a bit more text in the first major paragraph. 1/5/1/1 works, and so does 1/6/1/1. But once you start getting up into 1/7/1/1, you're asking a bit much of your reader—meaning they're less likely to make it through your introduction.

1/3/1 + 1/3/1

Now, let's say you need to write a hefty introduction.

(I use the word "need" very specifically here, because unless there's a real reason for your introduction to be longer than seven-or-so sentences, you should err on the side of brevity and kill a few more of your darlings.)

A "trick" for making a long introduction seem short is by repeating the first 1/3/1 structure over again, connecting them with a subhead.

Here's how it works:

> *This first sentence is your opener.*
>
> *This second sentence clarifies your opener. This third sentence reinforces the point you're making with some sort of credibility or amplified description. And this fourth sentence rounds out your argument.*
>
> *This fifth sentence is your conclusion.*
>
> *Now, here's a new first sentence as a second opener.*
>
> *And this second sentence clarifies your second opener. This third sentence reinforces the new point you're making—with some sort of credibility or amplified description. And this fourth sentence rounds out the second point of your argument.*
>
> *This fifth sentence is the big conclusion of your introduction.*

Now, unless you knew what to look for here, you might read a piece structured this way and think, "Well that's just a long introduction." But there's a lot happening beneath the surface that makes an introduction like this work—specifically how it moves the reader quickly down the page.

The other reason why repeating the 1/3/1 structure works so well is because it forces you, the writer, to be conscious and clear about what you're trying to accomplish in each section. Within the first five sentences of the piece, what are you trying to say? What's the one singular point you're trying to drive home? What's this story really about? And then, again in the second 1/3/1 section, what's the *new* point you're looking to drive home? Why is this also important to the reader? Does it really warrant having its own section?

Thinking in "chunks" like this is how you make your writing more potent.

And readers love writing that doesn't waste their time.

Here's an example of the 1/3/1 + 1/3/1 structure from my article, "8 Soft Skills You Need To Work At A High-Growth Startup."

> *It takes a certain type of personality to want to work at a startup — and the crucial qualities of startup employees you decide to hire.*

> *When I was 26 years old, one of my closest friends and I decided we were going to start a company. He was still in the process of finishing his MBA. I had recently taken the leap from my job as a copywriter working in advertising.*

And every few weeks he would fly to Chicago (where I was based), or I would fly to Atlanta (where he was based), and we'd trade off sleeping on each other's couches while brainstorming what our first step was going to be.

We called it Digital Press.

I'll never forget the day we decided to make our first hire.

He was a freelance writer recommended to me by a friend — and we were in the market to start hiring writers and editors (to replace the jobs my co-founder, Drew, and I were performing ourselves). We asked him to meet us at Soho House in Chicago, ordered a bottle of red wine to share, and "interviewed" him by the pool on the roof. He was a fiction writer with a passion for fantasy and sci-fi (not business writing, which was what we needed), and we were young and inexperienced just hoping someone would trust us enough to follow our vision.

We hired him — and fired him two months later.

The last thing I want to point out here is that you can actually make the 1/3/1 + 1/3/1 structure move even faster by combining the last sentence of the first section, and the first sentence of the second section, into one singular subhead.

Here's how it works:

This first sentence is your opener.

This second sentence clarifies your opener. This third sentence reinforces the point you're making with some sort of credibility or amplified description. And this fourth sentence rounds out your argument.

This fifth sentence is both your conclusion and the first sentence of your second section.

And this sixth sentence clarifies your second opener. This seventh sentence reinforces the new point you're making—with some sort of credibility or amplified description. And this eighth sentence rounds out the second point of your argument.

This ninth sentence is the big conclusion of your introduction.

Visually, this is so much easier to read. The subhead alone chops what could have been a very long introduction into a bunch of small, digestible bites—and the subhead grabs the reader's attention in a way that lets them know their first "milestone" is just a few sentences down. Writers who don't use subheads are significantly disadvantaged when it comes to writing online, because a reader's eyes naturally "look" for subheads more than they do full paragraphs and blocks of text.

Written content with no subheads feels exhausting.

On the other hand, lists with a lot of subheads feel easy and convenient.

1/3/1 + Bullets

Once you've mastered the basics of writing clean, organized, and rapid introductions, you can then start to step
out of the box and use other writing techniques to get
readers flying down the page.

For example, readers love bulleted lists.

This is a technique that works extremely well for your
Main Points, but there's also no reason why you can't use
it within your introduction as well. A bulleted list is just
a faster, more efficient way to cram a ton of value into
a very short amount of space. The key here isn't to list
things for listing's sake, but to think about what would
otherwise take five or more sentences to write, and to communicate that same information faster in a bulleted list.

Here's how it works:

This first sentence is your opener.

*This second sentence clarifies your opener. This third sen-
tence reinforces the point you're making with some sort of
credibility or amplified description. And this fourth sentence
rounds out your argument.*

*This fifth sentence is your conclusion, as well as the subhead
to your bulleted list.*

- *Point #1*
- *Point #2*
- *Point #3*
- *Point #4*
- *Etc.*

Now, bulleted lists can backfire when not used properly, so let me make this very clear. Lists, when combined with sub-par information, come off as weak, boring, and a waste of time. It's not the listing of things that readers enjoy. What they enjoy is being given a ton of valuable and relevant information in a compressed amount of time. Your job isn't to just "list" stuff. It's to take what otherwise would be a long-winded section and compress it using a different form or technique.

Here's an example of the 1/3/1 + Bullets structure from my article, "5 Serious Things You Should Know About Money Before You Turn 30."

> *Money, and "financial freedom," is a skill.*
>
> *No one ever tells you what you should know about money when you're young. There isn't a class in high school, or even college, where a professor sits you down and says, "Now listen up: mastering money is no different than learning how to shoot a basketball or paint a picture. It just takes practice."*
>
> *Instead, money remains (for many people) this massive unknown in their daily lives.*
>
> - *They don't know how to make more of it.*
> - *They don't know how to spend less of it.*
> - *They don't know how (they'll ever) save it.*
> - *And they don't know what to do with it once they have it.*
>
> *And that's a big problem.*

1 + Subhead

And finally, if you want to just get straight to the point, why waste any time?

One sentence is all you need in order to frame the piece—before immediately hitting the reader with the first milestone and subhead.

Here's how it works:

> *This first sentence is what the whole piece is about.*
>
> **And this first subhead is what we're going to dig into right here, right now.**

I don't recommend this technique for everything you write, but as a way to change things up, it can be a powerful mechanism for turning your Rate of Revelation knob to level 10.

Here's an example of the 1 + Subhead structure from my article, "I Used To Have Social Anxiety. These 4 Mental Shifts Made Me Confident."

> *Most people see confidence as something you're born with — you either have it or you don't.*
>
> **But the truth is, confidence is just like any other personality trait.**
>
> *If you want to be more patient, you have to practice patience. If you want to be more compassionate, you have to practice compassion. If you want to be more thoughtful, you have to*

practice doing things intentionally. And if you want to be confident, well then, you simply have to practice being confident.

The real strategy here is to make the reader feel like they've stepped into the middle of a piece by the time they've finished reading the very first sentence. There's something jarring (in a good way) about seeing the second sentence of an article bolded as a subhead. It tells the reader, "We're already getting to the good part," encouraging them to keep reading.

To Recap:

The types of introduction structures that work well are:

- 1/3/1
- 1/5/1
- 1/3/2/1
- 1/5/2/1
- 1/4/1/1
- 1/3/1 + 1/3/1
- 1/3/Subhead/3/1
- 1/3/1 + Bulleted List
- 1 + Subhead

Notice again how every single structure relies on a single opening sentence, and always ends with a single conclusion sentence. Pieces that open with two consecutive sentences in the first paragraph are weaker. And pieces that open with three or more sentences in the first paragraph are tiring for the reader. As much as possible, you want to crescendo and decrescendo your rhythms, starting with one sentence, then moving up to three, four, or five sentences, then back down to two sentences, then back down to one—and repeat.

This is what makes the reader feel like they're riding a wave.

And waves feel good.

The Art Of Writing Main Points

Once you've successfully framed what it is you're writing about, it's time to get into the Main Points of the piece.

Your Main Points are, quite literally, why the reader clicked on your headline to begin with. In fact, it's very common for readers to skim (or skip) the introduction of a piece and just start reading at the first Main Point. And it's even more common for readers to not even read the article in its entirety. What they'll do instead is skim the Main Points and subheads, and *then* decide whether it's worth going back and reading the article in full.

> If the "sweet spot" of an online article is 800 to 1,200 words, then your job as a writer is to pack as much value into your Main Points as possible—
> **without inflating the piece's word count.**

One of the biggest mistakes writers make when structuring their writing online is not thinking about how much "real estate" they're giving each point.

Which is why I encourage you to write backwards.

Once you've written your introduction (or, even before you write your introduction), skeleton out your piece by listing your Main Points. If you are writing an Opinion article, your Main Points are most likely going to be sentences and statements. If you are writing an Actionable Guide, your Main Points are going to be either sentences or categories. And if you are writing a Curated List, your Main Points are going to be the things you are listing: habits, lessons, movies, book titles, etc.

For example, here are the Main Points of my Opinion article, "Smart People Aren't Born Smart. They Do This, And Become Smart As A Result."

1. Smart people read (a lot).
2. Smart people hang around other smart people.
3. Smart people love making mistakes.
4. Smart people see value in all types of knowledge.
5. Smart people work (very, very) hard.

When I started writing this article, the first thing I did was write down these five Main Points. I wanted to have a sense of direction for the piece, and more importantly, to know how much space I needed to allocate for each point. As a rule of thumb, the more Main Points you have, the less explanation you are going to have for each one (in order to stay within the sweet spot of 800 to 1,200 words). Conversely, the less Main Points you have, the more explanation you are going to need in order for each point to stand securely on its own.

Let me repeat again:

- More Main Points = Less Explanation
- Less Main Points = More Explanation

Once you have the skeleton of your piece outlined, and you have a sense of how "big" (visually) each Main Point is going to be, the next step is to start filling them in.

1/2/5/3/1

For articles that have three or less Main Points, you are going to want to use a structure that doesn't cut your explanations too short.

The 1/2/5/3/1 structure is a good framework to use when thinking about how to make a solid argument for whatever it is you're writing about, without getting "lost in the sauce" and rambling on and on.

Here's how it works:

> *This first sentence is your opener.*
>
> *This second sentence clarifies your opener. And this third sentence is why the reader should care.*
>
> *This fourth sentence starts to expand on the point. This fifth sentence is a story, or some sort of credible piece of insight. This sixth sentence builds on that story or insight and tells the reader something they maybe didn't know. This seventh sentence is a small conclusion. And this eighth sentence is why that conclusion matters.*
>
> *This ninth sentence recaps what you just told the reader. This tenth sentence reinforces the argument you're making with an additional tidbit or insight. And this eleventh sentence drives the point home.*

This twelfth sentence reminds the reader of the important takeaway.

Looking at the above, you can then imagine what this entire piece would look like if each of your Main Points followed this same structure. Each section opens with a clear, declarative sentence. Each section ends with a clear declarative sentence. And the "bulk" of each section exists in the middle, where a reader doesn't feel like they're slogging through one long, dense paragraph after another.

Just so you can get a visual sense, here's how this structure looks if used within an article with three main points.

Main Point #1

This first sentence is your opener.

This second sentence clarifies your opener. And this third sentence is why the reader should care.

This fourth sentence starts to expand on the point. This fifth sentence is a story, or some sort of credible piece of insight. This sixth sentence builds on that story or insight and tells the reader something they maybe didn't know. This seventh sentence is a small conclusion. And this eighth sentence is why that conclusion matters.

This ninth sentence recaps what you just told the reader. This tenth sentence reinforces the argument you're making with an additional tidbit or insight. And this eleventh sentence drives the point home.

This twelfth sentence reminds the reader of the important takeaway.

Main Point #2

This first sentence is your opener.

This second sentence clarifies your opener. And this third sentence is why the reader should care.

This fourth sentence starts to expand on the point. This fifth sentence is a story, or some sort of credible piece of insight. This sixth sentence builds on that story or insight and tells the reader something they maybe didn't know. This seventh sentence is a small conclusion. And this eighth sentence is why that conclusion matters.

This ninth sentence recaps what you just told the reader. This tenth sentence reinforces the argument you're making with an additional tidbit or insight. And this eleventh sentence drives the point home.

This twelfth sentence reminds the reader of the important takeaway.

Main Point #3

This first sentence is your opener.

This second sentence clarifies your opener. And this third sentence is why the reader should care.

This fourth sentence starts to expand on the point. This fifth sentence is a story, or some sort of credible piece of insight. This sixth sentence builds on that story or insight and tells the reader something they maybe didn't know. This

*seventh sentence is a small conclusion. And this
eighth sentence is why that conclusion matters.*

*This ninth sentence recaps what you just told
the reader. This tenth sentence reinforces the
argument you're making with an additional
tidbit or insight. And this eleventh sentence
drives the point home.*

*This twelfth sentence reminds the reader of the
important takeaway.*

All of a sudden, whatever you're writing about feels
ultra-actionable. You know exactly how many Main Points
you want to cover. You know exactly how much explaining
you should do within each section. And if you want the
piece to be longer than 800 to 1,200 words, all you have
to do is keep adding Main Points, copy/pasting the same
structure within them.

1/3/1

Now, let's say you're writing about a topic with more than
three points.

Having more Main Points *does not* mean making the
piece longer. Your writing, no matter what genre you're
in, should not be longer for longer sake—ever. If anything,
you want to always be thinking the opposite. You should
be asking yourself, "How can I make this shorter? How can
I make this faster? How can I require less of the reader's
time?"

Speed is how you win on the internet.

As I mentioned above, the more Main Points you have in a piece, the less explanation you should give each point. This is where a structure like 1/3/1 works well—because it forces you, the writer, to make serious choices about what's worth saying and what's not.

Here's how it works:

This first sentence is your opener.

This second sentence clarifies your opener. And this third sentence is why the reader should care. This fourth sentence is your mini conclusion.

This fifth sentence is why that mini conclusion matters specifically to your target reader.

You can tell there is this massive leap that happens between the third and fourth sentences. Most writers here would continue describing or explaining whatever it is they're talking about. Instead, I encourage you to do the opposite. Skip right to the end. Tell the reader why this one specific Main Point matters to them, or what their take-away should be, and be done. Move on to the next point.

For example, here's the fast-paced 1/3/1 structure executed in my article, "12 Little Things That Show People You're Intelligent—Without You Having To Say It."

1. **Showing up on time.**

The most simple indicator of all.

If you are late, you are disrespectful. It doesn't matter the circumstance — unless the other party is luckily in the same boat (both of you enduring the same traffic). But still, it's always best to be the one on time.

Rule of thumb: if you're not early, you're late.

On its own, this paragraph might feel like it's lacking "depth." But what you have to remember is that for pieces that have five or more Main Points, the whole reason why a reader is there is because they want to know the Main Points themselves—not necessarily a dissertation on each one. In the above article, I have 12 Main Points. If I had explained each one in depth, chances are, readers would have opened the piece, started scrolling, and then said to themselves, "Jesus this is long," and then gone back to whatever it was they were doing before (probably watching cat videos).

So instead, I optimized the piece for the Main Points themselves. A reader could skim just the 12 bolded subheads of the piece and still extract "the Main Points."

Which is what happened.

That article went viral on Medium and accumulated over 250,000 views in less than 7 days.

1/1/1+

Now, let's say you want to move the reader along *even faster.*

Nothing moves a reader along better than a single sentence.

Nothing.

This structure is a popular one on the internet, however

it's also an easy one to abuse. A lot of writers who discover the power of this structure use it exclusively—and their writing ends up feeling over-caffeinated and monotone. Great writing, no matter how fast or slow, benefits from dynamics. You want to be staccato, and then you want to be legato. You want to crescendo, and then decrescendo.

Too much of any one rhythm is boring.

The 1/1/1+ structure is a mechanism you should use for very specific sections within your writing: beginnings and endings. Single sentences are great for calling out individual ideas, statements, or descriptions, and doing so several times in a row can elicit a powerful response in a reader.

Here's how it works:

This first sentence is a strong statement.

This second sentence builds on, reinforces, or repeats that strong statement.

This third sentence builds on, reinforces, or repeats that strong statement.

For example, I use this structure to emphasize a length of time in my article, "The 1 Thing I Did That Changed My Entire Life For The Better."

Step 2:

Like I said, I did this for 2 years.

Two. Years.

Not 3 days.

Not a few weeks.

*Two entire years. I started to see how the people
I was surrounding myself with weren't very
conducive to who and what I wanted to become.
I started to realize I was terrific at coming up
with ideas but horrible at seeing them through
to completion. I started to understand why
I struggled to make friends, and how closed off
I was from the world.*

If you notice, immediately following the 1/1/1/1 structure,
I went into a lengthier paragraph. This was deliberate.
When you use the 1/1/1+ structure, you are building
momentum. You are moving a reader quickly from Point A
to Point B. But after a few big steps, the reader is not going
to want to run anymore. They're going to want to take a
quick break and settle into the thing you're talking about.
So, crescendo with the 1/1/1+ rhythm, and then decrescendo with a three, four, or even five-sentence paragraph.

Then repeat.

Main Point / 1, 2, or 3

Finally, let's say you are writing a piece with twenty Main
Points.

Again, unless you are intentionally trying to write a massive Ultimate Guide that requires twenty Main Points and
in-depth explanations for all of them, you are going to
want to optimize your writing for readers who are there to
skim. That said, I can't stress enough how important it is
for the writing beneath each Main Point to still hold value.
Just because you only have two sentences to make a point,

doesn't mean those two sentences are worthless. If anything, you should be asking how you can make those two sentences as impactful as possible—with the understanding that some readers are only going to read your bolded Main Points.

Here's how it works:

You have your Main Point here.

And then you have one, two, or three sentences (max) expanding on that Main Point.

That's it.

Because you have to think: if you are aiming to write a 1,000 word article, and you have twenty Main Points, that means each point can only have 50 words—and that's not counting your introduction, or any sort of conclusion.

Which is why I encourage you to skeleton your pieces and list out your Main Points before you begin.

For example, I use this structure in my article, "20 Things Nobody Tells You About Growing Up."

1. **Most people are scared of imagination**

They've disconnected with their inner child. They don't feel they are "creative." They like things "just the way they are."

2. **Your dream doesn't really matter to anyone else.**

Some people might take interest. Some may support you in your quest. But at the end of the

day, nobody cares, or will ever care about your
dream as much as you.

3. Friends are relative to where you are in your life.

Most friends only stay for a period of time —
usually in reference to your current interest. But
when you move on, or your priorities change, so
too do the majority of your friends.

In articles like these, it's the Main Points that are the most valuable parts of the entire piece.

Remember, the reason why a reader chose to click on this headline was because they cared about the "20 Things." So, I spent a significant amount of time refining each Main Point to be highly relevant to the reader and topic at hand. If my Main Points had been broad, vague words instead, I guarantee this article wouldn't have performed as well as it did (300,000 views across *Inc Magazine*, Quora, and Medium).

Take a look:

1. Imagination

They've disconnected with their inner child. They don't
feel they are "creative." They like things "just the way
they are."

2. Dream

Some people might take interest. Some may support you
in your quest. But at the end of the day, nobody cares,
or will ever care about your dream as much as you.

3. Friends

Most friends only stay for a period of time — usually in reference to your current interest. But when you move on, or your priorities change, so too do the majority of your friends.

A style like this (where the subheads are just individual words) is actually much harder for a reader to skim.

The reason is because the Main Points don't really give "the answer" they came looking for ("What are the 20 Things?"). Instead, they're forced to take an extra step and actually read each point in detail. And I can hear a lot of crusty old writers shouting, "Yes! God forbid a reader actually reads the damn thing!" But as the young whippersnapper in the room here, I have to be the bearer of bad news and point out: how you get readers online to *actually* read what you wrote in the first place is by hooking their attention.

Otherwise, they aren't even going to get past your first Main Point.

Bolded Statements

Now, let's say you aren't writing something that is a numbered list.

All of these same mechanics, structures, and rhythms still apply. Instead of thinking of your Main Points in terms of a list, think of them in terms of individual statements. What's the next "new" piece of information you can reveal to the reader? And how can you emphasize certain statements, insights, or stories to drive home the purpose of the piece?

Writers *severely* underestimate how powerful subheads are in the world of online writing. If you don't use subheads, you're at a disadvantage simply because readers on the internet specifically look for bolded, highlighted, emphasized pieces of the story. Why? Because these feel like shortcuts. They're candy. A bolded sentence subconsciously tells a reader, "I'm not going to waste your time. Something important is happening here."

When executed perfectly, the same way a reader could skim all the Main Points of an article and feel like they "got it," a reader should be able to skim all the bolded subheads and sentences within a piece and feel like they "got it."

For example, here's an introduction that uses subheads to push a reader along quickly, in my article, "How I Spend My Free Time Is Why I Am Successful."

> *Invest in yourself.*
>
> *The other day, I was chatting with a friend of a friend, a senior in high school who was getting ready to go off to college.*
>
> *"I want to start my life over," he said. "I want to reinvent myself, and prove that you don't have to follow the same path as everyone else."*
>
> *"You can do that," I said. "But you have to be willing to do 1 thing that not very many teenagers and young adults are willing to do."*
>
> *"What's that?" he asked.*
>
> **You have to spend more time learning outside of class, than you do in class.**

This goes for anyone in school, out of school, young, old, whatever. You're either in class, or you're at work.

During those hours, you can learn. You can grow. You can improve certain skills. You can even make money.

But anyone who truly makes something of themselves sees that time as their daily standard. But they do not see it as "the end." They do not get out of class, or leave work and think, "Ah, time to sit back, relax, and just chill."

No. They take that "free time" and they reinvest it in themselves.

They work on a side project.

They practice their craft.

They improve their skills, or study, or spend time learning from people far more knowledgeable.

Had I not bolded these sentences, this piece would have been read completely differently. In fact, it's the way these sentences are separated out and highlighted that gives them so much power. Had I just buried them within a paragraph, they would have lost a lot of their weight.

Take a look:

The other day, I was chatting with a friend of a friend, a senior in high school who was getting ready to go off to college. "I want to start my life over," he said. "I want to reinvent myself, and prove that you don't have to follow the same path as everyone else."

"You can do that," I said. "But you have to be willing to do 1 thing that not very many teenagers and young adults are willing to do."

"What's that?" he asked.

You have to spend more time learning outside of class, than you do in class. This goes for anyone in school, out of school, young, old, whatever. You're either in class, or you're at work. During those hours, you can learn. You can grow. You can improve certain skills. You can even make money. But anyone who truly makes something of themselves sees that time as their daily standard. But they do not see it as "the end." They do not get out of class, or leave work and think, "Ah, time to sit back, relax, and just chill."

The content is exactly the same, but because it's structured differently, you read it differently.

Which is why there is so much power in understanding the *visual* nature of online writing, and how you can use these signals to your advantage—to hook and keep a reader's attention.

Once you understand the basics of creating a skeleton of your Main Points, and expanding or contracting the amount of explanation for each, you can then start to make up your own structures and rhythms.

Here are a few more that I use often.

Short / Long / Long / Short

Thinking of structure in terms of sentence length is only the beginning. You have a lot more room to play in if you think of total paragraph length instead.

For example, here's an excerpt from my article, "Disciplined People Who Achieve Their Goals Live By These 7 Habits."

> *Anyone can make a list of goals—but only a few learn how to be disciplined enough to achieve them.*
>
> *I grew up in a home and a family that constantly reinforced the importance of self-discipline. Every single night, I'd watch my dad set the timer on the coffee maker and put his oatmeal in the refrigerator for the next morning. By 5:30 a.m., he'd be awake. By 6:00 a.m., he'd be in the gym. By 7:00 a.m., he'd be knocking on my bedroom door, making sure I was awake. And by 8:00 a.m., he'd be at the hospital ready to operate. My dad is a spine surgeon.*
>
> *My mom, meanwhile, somehow managed to work as a voice teacher at a local college, and take my sister to her violin lessons, and take my younger brother to gymnastics practice, and take my other younger brother to chess club, all while making sure dinner was on the table by 5:00 p.m., and everyone was working on their homework or practicing their respective musical instrument by 7:00 p.m.*

Our house operated like a retreat for the arts with my mother's thumb on a stopwatch.

Paragraphs two and three in this excerpt are nearly the same size—and yet the second paragraph is six sentences and paragraph three is one very long sentence.

There are a few things to take note of here.

First, you never want to have three or more long paragraphs one after another. That style of writing has been dead for years, and anyone writing that way on the internet is clinging to a way things were but no longer are.

Second, if you *are* going to have long paragraphs one after another, you want to find ways to change up their internal rhythm so they don't feel or sound exactly the same. One way of doing this is by using punctuation. Have one paragraph with a lot of short, strong sentences. Have the next paragraph be one long, winding sentence.

This is what makes them seem "different."

Lastly, notice how before and after both long paragraphs in the above excerpt there are single, declarative sentences. This is very intentional. Again, you want to subtly tell the reader, "I'm going to tell you a quick story—this will only take a second," before giving them their next mile marker. There's something about reading a single sentence after a long paragraph that gives a reader the same feeling a listener gets hearing a chord resolve on the piano.

Let your chords resolve.

Repetition

Repetition is a common mechanism in poetry.

But that doesn't mean it can't be used in other forms of writing.

One of the best ways to avoid spending unnecessary time explaining things to a reader is to use repetition as a way of advancing your Rate of Revelation. Think of repetition as a bulleted list, but in prose form.

For example, here's an excerpt from my article, "How Do Some People Succeed So Quickly? They Approach Life Like This."

1. **Every single moment, of every single day, you are "practicing" something.**

   If you don't floss in the morning, you're practicing not-flossing.

   If you choose to eat quinoa and veggies instead of Frosted Flakes, you're practicing eating for fuel instead of eating for enjoyment.

   If you yell at your significant other, you're practicing a lack of self-control.

   If you watch TV instead of working on your book, you're practicing postponing your dream of becoming a novelist.

   The moment you start to see the world this way, you start to realize that every single moment, of every single day, you are practicing something.

And how aware you are of whatever it is you're practicing dictates how consciously (or unconsciously) you move toward or away from where it is you actually want to be: whether that's a destination, a physical place, or an emotional state.

Here, I am combining the 1/1/1/1 structure with repetition to give a reader plenty of actionable examples without forcing them to read through paragraphs of prose. I'm only giving them what they absolutely need—and then once I've given them a handful of examples, I follow up with a longer, more descriptive paragraph (alternating rhythms).

First, Second, etc.

There's a subtle difference in voice between an article that "lists" two points, compared to one that emphasizes point one, and then point two. Now, will numbering vs "saying" your points make or break the performance of your piece? Probably not. But these small details are the types of things you should be constantly questioning in your writing.

For example, here's an excerpt from my article, "You Stop Being Productive The Moment You Do This."

Contrary to popular belief, there is such a thing as being "too productive."

I like to think about this in two ways:

First, you are being "too productive" the moment that your input becomes disproportionate to your output.

Let's use writing as an example.

I know a good many writers who feel all sorts of productive simply because of how many books they're able to read in a day, week, month, or year.

Now, let's say you are an incredibly productive reader. You are able to read pages and pages without effort. You are able to retain a significant amount of the material you consume. When it comes to reading, you are an absolute professional.

The problem is, your "Chief Aim," your GOAL, isn't to become a master reader (maybe that's a tangential goal, but it's not your main goal). Your goal is to become a writer. And while reading is certainly an important part of writing, and become a professional writer, the moment your input becomes disproportionate to your output, you are no longer being productive. Because while you may be turning into an incredibly effective reader, there is a tipping point where "more reading" isn't going to move you any further along as a writer.

So, the "act" can be productive, but unless the "act" is aligned with the GOAL, then it wouldn't be accurate to say your ACTIONS (as a whole) are productive.

That's the first example.

The second example of being "too productive" is when your productivity has a disproportionate impact on your quality of life.

In order to achieve anything great in life, you will have to make sacrifices.

It would be naive to think that you could achieve the highest levels of success (or "productivity") without some compromise: letting go of certain relationships, eating less healthfully, sleeping less, enduring high amounts of stress, etc. Whatever that compromise becomes is up to you, but somewhere, somehow, your drive toward your "Chief Aim" will cause you to have to ignore other aspects of your life.

However, there's a tipping point here as well.

The moment your drive puts you in the hospital, you know you have a problem. The moment your significant other sits you down and says, "I can't keep seeing you like this," you know you've gone too far. The variables of life can bend, but at a certain point, they can and they will snap. And it's up to you to figure out how far you can bend before you break.

By crafting each Main Point as a statement, instead of just a two-point list, the piece feels like you're speaking directly to the reader. They can hear the emphasis in the voice. They can feel the power of what's being said, and understand why these two (specific) Main Points are delivering on the PROMISE made in the headline.

There's also an element of repetition here, writing out "first" and "second" in the subheads. There was also repetition in the very first example I used, each subhead stating, "Smart People X, Smart People Y, Smart People Z." There's something about repetition in subheads that tells the reader, "This piece was very intentionally organized," again reinforcing that you are credible, that you know what you're doing, and that you're the right person they should be reading on this particular topic.

Look at the way I've structured this chapter:

- The Art Of Writing Introductions
- The Art Of Writing Main Points
- The Art Of Writing Conclusions

Repetition.

Bold ½ Sentences

This is one of my favorite, and yet one of the least used mechanisms in online writing.

Combine repetition with bolding the first half of your sentences.

The whole idea here is to do nothing but emphasize the structure you're using to your readers. So much of online writing is about signaling—signaling this piece is easy to read, signaling you know what you're doing, signaling it's fun and there's a voice and rhythm here worth paying attention to (see how even in this sentence, I've repeated the word "signaling" multiple times?).

For example, here's an excerpt from my article, "This 1 Tip Changed My Writing Forever."

> **A few months after that, he'd quit the game and I was one of the highest-ranked players in the entire country.**
>
> *That lesson is, to date, one of the most influential pieces of advice I've ever received as a human being. That was the first time someone I looked up to, someone I wanted to "be like," told me that no amount of me watching or idolizing someone else was going to replace the hard work I needed to put in myself.*
>
> *When I started my gaming blog as a teenager, I implemented that same mentality. I didn't really read anyone else's blog. I didn't "consume." I just wrote. And wrote. And wrote. Every single night before bed, I pushed myself to write 1 new blog post for the following morning. And by the time I showed up for my first journalism class, Freshman year of college, I had 10,000 gamers reading my blog every single day — an unheard of accomplishment in 2009, back when blogging was considered "weird."*
>
> *When I quit gaming and started bodybuilding, I applied this same mentality again. I didn't spend hours and hours watching other people lift online. I went to the gym and lifted myself. And I transformed from a 110 pound, awkward, skinny teenager, to a 170 pound shredded fitness model.*

When I stopped bodybuilding and started really nurturing my craft for writing, I did it again. *I wrote 1 answer every single day here on Quora for almost 3 years in a row. I wrote 400+ columns for Inc Magazine. I ghostwrote nearly 1,000 articles for CEOs and founders and investors and public speakers. And every single night, I worked on my first book, Confessions of a Teenage Gamer. I didn't sit in my room and consume other people's writing for hours and hours. I practiced my writing instead.*

In this story, each one of these paragraphs is covering a different period of time.

If I had crammed them all together, the reader would have felt overwhelmed, and maybe even lost. They'd have said to themselves, "Wait, what do gaming and bodybuilding and writing have to do with each other? Why are you jumping around so much?"

To combat that confusion, I chose to separate each "chapter," and then bold the first half of the sentence to signal to the reader, "In this paragraph we're talking about gaming. In this paragraph we're talking about bodybuilding. And in this paragraph we're talking about writing." All of a sudden, this small tweak makes the reader feel like they have a firm sense of what they're reading and how it's being organized.

The key, however, is to tie the bolded sentence to one paragraph and one paragraph only.

A less effective way of using this mechanism would look like this.

When I started my gaming blog as a teenager,
I implemented that same mentality. I didn't
really read anyone else's blog. I didn't "consume."
I just wrote.

And wrote. And wrote.

Every single night before bed, I pushed myself to
write 1 new blog post for the following morning.
And by the time I showed up for my first jour-
nalism class, Freshman year of college, I had
10,000 gamers reading my blog every single day
— an unheard of accomplishment in 2009, back
when blogging was considered "weird."

When I quit gaming and started bodybuild-
ing, *I applied this same mentality again.*

I didn't spend hours and hours watching other
people lift online. I went to the gym and lifted
myself. And I transformed from a 110 pound,
awkward, skinny teenager, to a 170 pound
shredded fitness model.

When I stopped bodybuilding and started
really nurturing my craft for writing, *I did it*
again. I wrote 1 answer every single day here on
Quora for almost 3 years in a row.

I wrote 400+ columns for Inc Magazine.

I ghostwrote nearly 1,000 articles for CEOs and
founders and investors and public speakers.

And every single night, I worked on my first book,
Confessions of a Teenage Gamer. I didn't sit in

my room and consume other people's writing for
hours and hours. I practiced my writing instead.

By separating the paragraphs out, the general concept still "works," it's just not nearly as effective.

The strategy behind bolding the first half of a sentence is to signal to the reader, "This sentence, *and this entire paragraph*, are one section."

The Art Of Writing Conclusions

Conclusions are tricky.

In stories, particularly fiction but also nonfiction as well, the conclusion of the story is known as the "descending action." The climax has already happened—the wall was torn down, the war was officially won (or lost), the main character's love interest died, etc.—and now the reader needs to know how things ended up. What was the result of this story's climax?

Inherently, any descending action is going to be less interesting than the ascending action that came before it. There's momentum, anticipation, and suspense in ascending action. Descending action is more about reflection and meaningful takeaways. And these can still be interesting story elements to the reader, but there's a reason why the ascending action was 200 pages and the descending action was the last 30 pages of the book.

Once the climax happens, the reader is "done."

When it comes to online writing, conclusions are optional.

The truth is, readers don't need them.

Especially in an 800 to 1,200-word article, a conclusion should happen in the span of a paragraph—or even a single sentence. Your last Main Point is technically the "climax" of the piece. And if we know anything about digital readers, it's that as soon as they're "done," they're done. They've already swiped back to their feed and started looking for the next piece of content to give their time and attention.

Here are a handful of rhythms you can use to craft effective conclusions.

The Cliff

One of the best ways to get a reader to read another piece of your writing is to leave them with a massive cliffhanger.

This type of structure works well with Curated Lists, where the entire purpose of the piece is for you to list Main Points that speak to the reader's interests. In these types of pieces, the reader doesn't need a big, fancy conclusion. They got what they came for and they're happy you delivered on that PROMISE.

So, as soon as you finish your last Main Point, jump off the cliff.

Don't even say goodbye.

For example, here's the last Main Point from my article, "30 Things You Should Know About Life Before You Turn 30."

30. Ten years is a very long time.

When I was 19, 20 years old, I wanted to be a rapper.

When I was 21, 22, 23, I wanted to be a bodybuilder.

When I was 24, 25, 26, I wanted to be a creative director at a huge advertising agency.

When I was 27, 28, 29, I wanted to be an entrepreneur.

And from age 17 to 29, I've wanted to be a writer.

In my 20s, I got to live 4 completely different lives. I immersed myself in 4 different industries, learned entire tool kits of different skills, made different friends, explored different paths, and ultimately became different versions of myself.

And every one of those pursuits made me who I am "today."

If I was able to live that many different lives in those ten years, then I can only imagine what 30 to 40 will look like, and how many different lives I may be able to live again.

Ten years is a long time. And the older you get,

the more knowledge you accumulate, the more
resources you have, and the more freedom in
front of you to become whatever it is you want
to become.

I don't feel old at 30.

I feel like I'm just getting started.

Here, I deliberately wrote the last Main Point of the piece
to stick within the structure of all the other Main Points,
but also "sound" like a conclusion. There's no all-
encompassing takeaway. There's no whole other section
explaining to the reader why what they just read matters.
My PROMISE was, "30 Things You Should Know About Life
Before You Turn 30." I delivered on that PROMISE.
And now we're done.

However, even if your last Main Point doesn't have
a nuanced conclusion, this technique can still work well.

For example, here's how I end my article, "Successful
People Tell Themselves These 7 Things On A Daily Basis."

7. "Never forget why you started."

Again, I am constantly surprised by people who
have achieved massive amounts of success in
their lives, and how connected they are to the
beginning of their journey.

They remember where they started. They remind
themselves often why they got into the business
they're in. Their motivation comes from a love
for growth, not necessarily the achievement of
an end goal.

In order to maintain long-term success, this is a crucial part of the process. You have to remember why you started down this road in the first place — and do everything in your power to make sure you never forget it.

As a reader, if you finished reading this article and felt yourself wanting more, you would need to click to read another one of my articles.

That's the whole point of The Cliff.

The Extended Final Main Point

Another way you can end a piece is by baking your mini conclusion into the very last Main Point.

Instead of starting a whole new section, just extend your final thoughts with an extra paragraph or sentence. Elaborate not just on the Main Point you were making, but on the meaningful takeaways from all your Main Points in the piece.

For example, I use the Extended Final Main Point structure in this article, "7 Questions You Should Ask Yourself To Become A Better Person."

7. "How can I be more helpful — to those around me, and to myself?"

It's taken me a long time to learn that if you can't spend all your time trying to make everyone around you happy.

You have to prioritize keeping yourself happy too.

Which is why it's worth questioning both, simultaneously.

What can you do to be more helpful to those around you? How can you be more encouraging, more patient? And at the same time, how can you do those same things toward yourself?

Personal development is an ongoing practice. It's not a destination. It's not something you do once and then you're a "perfect person" for the rest of your life.

Personal development is your ability to continuously ask yourself these questions on a daily basis, and slowly improve over time.

Like water over rocks, who you are is sculpted over years and years.

If you read closely, the final Main Point ends and the conclusion begins with the sentence, "Personal development is an ongoing practice."

As a reader, there's no clear indicator they've exited the last Main Point and suddenly entered the conclusion—which is good. The reader then gets the benefit of *feeling* like the piece has a nice neat bow on top, without needing to slog through a whole other section repeating everything that came before it (which most readers will just skim through anyway).

The Summary

The Summary technique works particularly well within Actionable Guide articles, or very long pieces with lots of different sections.

Readers appreciate summaries. There's a reason why every self-help or business book ends each chapter with a "recap" or page of "action steps." Especially when you're covering a lot of ground, or a topic requires a lot of additional explanation, summaries are a way for you to make sure you and the reader are on the same page (pun intended) before moving on to the next Main Point.

For example, I use a bulleted summary as the conclusion of my article, "You Stop Being Productive The Moment You Start Doing This."

> **The art of "being productive," then, is all about balancing the following variables:**
>
> - *Input as it relates to output (you should be "doing" more than you're "consuming")*
>
> - *Productivity weighed against the sustainable aspects of your life (mental, physical, emotional, and spiritual health)*
>
> - *Driving the highest impact for the lowest amount of effort (prioritizing what's truly going to "move the needle" over what doesn't move the needle but feels urgent)*
>
> *Finding this sweet spot is the reason why some people do incredible things with our universal*

24-hour clock, and others do almost nothing.

Instead of re-stating everything I had said earlier in the piece, I recapped the Main Points in a bulleted list to make the reader feel like they had the Sparknotes version—with one single sentence at the very end as an all-encompassing conclusion. You can also imagine how you could use this technique at the end of an introduction, or even at the end of any of your Main Points to help the reader follow along more closely.

Readers love checklists, action steps, quick recaps, small reminders, etc., so the more you can use these techniques to your advantage, the easier it will be for them to understand precisely what it is you're trying to tell them.

Strong Opinion

If you're going to take the time to end a piece with some sort of complete conclusion, I encourage you to make it a Strong Opinion.

There's nothing more boring to a reader than writing that re-says what it just said. A great conclusion is one that drives home a *new* point, or makes it very clear why someone should or shouldn't do something. Actionable advice, or an unexpected insight, are things that make the reader feel like the conclusion is another Main Point, just speaking a bit more holistically.

For example, this is the conclusion in my Opinion article, "Why Gary Vaynerchuk's Perspective On Meditation Is Everything That's Wrong With Mindfulness In Entrepreneurship."

Stop trying to 'unlock' yourself for the sake of achievement.

As Vaynerchuk says often, "I don't know what will happen once I buy the Jets. I don't actually want to buy the Jets. I'm in love with the hustle. The Game."

And what happens when that game stops? When you can no longer escape into the endlessly fun pursuit of mastering the rules, overcoming obstacles, and proving yourself among your competitors? What happens when you've bought the new "meditation drink" and you're bored of wearing your "meditation clothes" and you've eaten at all the nearby "meditation-friendly food spots."

The dust will settle. You will find yourself in silence.

And in that uncomfortable moment, with nothing else to achieve, you will be left with only yourself.

THAT, is the purpose of meditation. And I encourage every — not just entrepreneur, but human being — to make time for that practice.

What makes this an effective conclusion is that the advice, "Stop trying to 'unlock' yourself for the sake of achievement" could be a Main Point in itself.

This is why I'm such a big believer in The Cliff as a writing mechanism for the internet. Everything you write should, in some sense, feel like both a stand-alone piece *and* a piece within your larger library. You *want* readers to want more from you. You *want* them to feel like you cut them off right when momentum was high. You *want* them clicking to read more and more and more of your stuff—without them feeling tricked or dragged along.

Lazy writers do this by saying things like, "Which is why, if you want to know more, you should check out my website, and if you want to hear what I really think about this topic, you should check out my YouTube," blah blah blah.

Readers hate that shit.

Instead, just say what you want to say in this one individual piece, and be done. Let there be some dissonance in the air. Let readers feel like you could have said more, but didn't.

This is what gets them to come back again and again.

Language Rules

The last thing I want to touch on here is about language.

All of these structures and rhythms I've outlined for you will be read in very different ways depending on the type of language you choose within your writing. For example, "Dareth I say thou art but a reader of mine?" is a completely different language set than, "Do you want to read something I wrote?"

As a rule of thumb: readers on the internet don't like complicated.

Sure, you can make the argument that you're a professor or

a scientist and readers within your niche care very much about density of language, but even still, I would remind you of the context in which they are reading. There's a massive cognitive difference between scrolling through status updates in your Facebook feed versus reading an in-depth analysis on the future of blockchain technology. And since most readers use these candy-like social environments to discover new pieces of writing online, they are going to feel the mental difference between reading, "Oh my God, if I hear about the Kardashians I'm going to lose my mind" and "Zk-SNARKs are trustless zero-knowledge proof systems."

I'm not advocating for dumbing your writing down.

I'm advocating for making deliberate choices to make your writing sound more natural.

Here are a few writing rules I encourage you to live by:

- **Write for the everyday person.** If you are hell-bent on writing at an academic level, realize you are writing for a considerably smaller audience—which means, by definition, your material will almost never be read by the masses. If what you want is broad exposure, then it's important for you to use non-complicated language. For example, don't use semicolons (very few people understand how they work anyway). If there's a simpler synonym for a word less than 10% of society knows the definition to, use it. (Why? Because most people don't use words like, "prodigious" or "confounding" when they speak. They just say, "Wow that was amazing.")

- **Write how you speak.** Record yourself talking about a topic and then transcribe the recording. Pay close attention to the rhythm of your natural sentences, versus the rhythms you try to use when writing to "sound" more professional in your writing. As a rule of thumb, anyone who *tries* to sound professional ends up sounding inauthentic, and those who lean into their authentic voice end up being perceived as the most relatable.

- **Avoid long sentences.** Unless you're using one long sentence stylistically, like to counterbalance a paragraph of many short sentences, you should err on the side of brevity. The more winding your thoughts, the more confusing your writing will be for the reader to follow. Remember, you are writing for someone whose eyes are flying across the page at lightspeed.

- **Alternate sentence length.** If you read your article and find most of your sentences and paragraphs are all the same length, you have a rhythm problem. Short sentences should be followed by longer sentences. Longer sentences should be followed by short sentences. Short paragraphs should be followed by long paragraphs, and really long paragraphs should be followed by really short paragraphs. As Mozart said, "Music is not in the notes, but in the silence between."

- **Write confidently and declaratively.** A lot of people hesitate to "make a point" or "take a stance" when writing online because they don't want to get criticized in the comments. As a result, their writing stands for nothing, and resonates with no one. It's safe. It's self-conscious. And worst of all, it's vague. The more declarative you can be with your language, the more you will force readers to make a decision. Either they will say, "I strongly agree," or they will say, "I strongly disagree." Either of these responses is far better than, "Meh."

Chapter 9

How To Talk About Yourself Without Making Your Writing All About "You"

Self-promotion on the internet follows the rule of opposites.

- The more you promote yourself, the less people listen.
- The less you promote yourself, the more people listen.

Companies and industry leaders make this mistake constantly, as do aspiring writers and storytellers. They want people to know who they are, and so they write exclusively about their company or themselves. They want people to know about their new product, so they promote its benefits and features. In reality, people don't care about either. People, especially consumers, only care about their own interests and desires. If you can speak directly to those interests and desires, then you can attract them as customers. If you can't, then no amount of shouting from the rooftops is going to make them pay attention.

You are not the main character in your story.
The reader is.

There is a nuance in what I am saying here.

I am not advocating for never talking about yourself, your company, or any of your products for sale. In fact, talking about yourself, or the success of your products can oftentimes be important context and credibility for the reader. For example, if I am reading a piece about real estate trends, and the author of the piece says in the introduction, "I am the founder of a multi-billion-dollar real estate firm," that's going to help me trust the opinions and insights being shared. The same goes for someone talking about their new book. If they let me, the reader, know this is their 8th *New York Times* best-selling book, that's going to give me important context as to the credibility of the information being shared with me.

Unfortunately, a lot of writers shy away from talking about themselves in this way. I run into this with executives I work with who hesitate sharing any of their own personal experiences out of fear of coming off too "self-promotional." What they fail to realize, however, is how much the reader actually wants to hear about these personal experiences. There's just a difference between talking about yourself *simply because you want to talk about yourself,* and talking about yourself *for the purpose of giving important context to the reader.*

This is what I like to call The Golden Intersection.

The Golden Intersection is the single most effective way of talking about yourself without being self-promotional.

If I tell you I am a 4x Top Writer on Quora with tens of millions of views on my writing, and that's the only thing I tell you, then I seem like a self-centered egomaniac.

But if I tell you I'm a 4x Top Writer on Quora with tens of millions of views on my writing, and I want to tell *you* how *you can become a Top Writer with tens of millions of views on your own writing too,* suddenly I don't seem self-promotional. I'm just letting you know where my insights are coming from, and that I'm a credible source of information.

The difference between the former and the latter is that in the first example, I am the main character. I'm who is important, and I'm banking on the reader taking an interest in me.

In the latter, I am no longer the main character.

You are.

I'm telling *you* how *you* can achieve *your* goal of becoming a Top Writer on Quora—and, for context, here's how I became a Top Writer on Quora myself.

The Golden Intersection of great writing is:
Answering The Reader's Question x Telling Them An Entertaining Story

Whenever you are talking about yourself, it should be done in a way that gives necessary context to the reader.

- If you're writing about how to learn a skill, you should also tell the reader how you learned that skill.

- If you're writing about what it feels like to fall out of love, you should also tell the reader about a time you fell out of love.

- If you're writing about the future of technology, you should also tell the reader about the history of technology and what you've experienced in the past.

- If you're writing about politics, you should also tell the reader how you got involved in politics.

The Golden Intersection puts the reader's wants, needs, questions, and desires as the #1 priority. This article is about how *you* can learn a certain skill. This story is about how *you* are feeling falling out of love. This piece is about how *you* should be thinking about the future of technology. *You, you, you.*

Then, to give context to the information, and to make the examples feel more relatable, I (as the writer) should let you know where this information is coming from. This article is about how *you* can learn a certain skill, "...and how I learned that skill was by practicing for four hours, every single day." This story is about how *you* are feeling falling out of love," ...and I know, because when I was 25 years old, I fell out of love too." This piece is about how *you* should be thinking about the future of technology," ...and that's because I've interviewed hundreds of technologists over the past few years."

The Art of Promoting Yourself

Now, let's say you want to promote a product.

For example, you just wrote a book titled, "Green At Home: How To Grow Your Own Vegetable Farm In Your Kitchen (For Less Than $50 Per Month)," and you want everybody to know about it. To get some exposure on the book, you decide to start authoring articles on the internet, directing readers to buy the paperback copy on Amazon.

Here's what most authors (including the ones signed with major publishing houses) do:

- **The author writes their very first piece on Medium or Quora and then gets frustrated when millions of people don't immediately read what they wrote.** "I'm a successful writer," they say to themselves. "More people should be reading my writing. This platform must be broken."

- **The author then hires a PR firm to get columnists to write about the wisdom being shared in their new book.** The PR firm has to then fight an uphill battle because most columnists know readers don't want to read an entire article about a product—readers only care about their own questions, needs, and desires. When the PR firm does finally get someone to write about the book, the piece gets less than 1,000 views because it's a promotional piece (and again, nobody wakes up in the morning excited to read an advertisement).

- **The author finally decides to take matters into their own hands and start writing on their blog.** "Fine, I'll do this myself!" they shout. They write a blog post titled, "The Book You Need To Read This Summer About Growing Your Own Vegetable

Farm." On some level, the author intuitively understands they need to write for their audience, they just aren't sure how to do that consciously. And even if they get the title right, they end up writing an entire piece filled with salesy language trying very hard to get the reader to go to Amazon and click "purchase."

The Golden Intersection is the answer to all of these problems.

The problem here is that "the product" is being treated as the main character.

Instead, a more effective way of approaching The Golden Intersection would be to write about all the mistakes *you* make when trying to start *your own* farm at home—and then telling readers how you (the author) made those same mistakes early on too. Or, writing about the amazing life lessons that can be learned by farming your own vegetables at home, and then telling the stories of how you (the author) learned those same life lessons by farming your own vegetables at home too.

The Golden Intersection puts the reader first.

- This piece is about their questions.
- This piece is about their wants and needs.
- This piece is about their desires.

When you put the reader first, suddenly the moments you talk about yourself aren't really about yourself—they're visual examples of the points you're making for the reader's benefit. You're telling a story that is *showing* the answer to the reader's question.

Here are a few examples of pieces you could write to "promote" this book:

- 7 Mistakes People Make When Trying To Grow Vegetables At Home For The First Time

- How To Grow Tomatoes In Your Own Kitchen For Under $50 Per Month: 3 Easy Steps

- The 1 Unforgettable Life Lesson You'll Learn As Soon As You Stop Going Grocery Shopping—And Start Growing Your Own Food

Each of these titles speaks to a particular pain point the reader might be experiencing: a question they have, a result they want, a lifestyle they desire. Then, within each one of these pieces, you can (and should) talk about how *you* learned the very same thing the reader is looking to learn, so the reader can better imagine themselves moving forward on their own path.

> The single most effective way to "promote" yourself without promoting yourself is to use **you, your company, or your product as context** to the thing you're explaining to the reader.

For example, let's say you're writing the piece, "7 Mistakes People Make When Trying To Grow Vegetables At Home For The First Time."

In the third or fourth Main Point of the piece, you might say:

> *"The fourth mistake people make is they start with too many different vegetables. I tell this story at length in my new book, "Green At Home: How To Grow Your Own Vegetable Farm In Your Kitchen (For Less Than $50 Per Month)," but the first time I tried growing veggies in my kitchen, I ended up spending hundreds of dollars. I made the mistake of thinking the same strategies that applied to growing tomatoes could be used to grow zucchini and carrots and microgreens, etc. I ended up learning (the hard way) this is not the case."*

The very first sentence of this above paragraph is the most important one.

By first speaking directly to the reader's questions, fears, etc.—"The fourth mistake people make is they start with too many different vegetables"—any story you start telling thereafter is going to be seen as a reinforcement of that lesson or insight. The reader doesn't feel like you're rambling. The reader feels like you're giving them context for how you learned this same lesson yourself.

As a result, the piece reaches a wider number of readers (because it's positioned as an answer to the target reader's question).

Here's a different example.

Let's say you're the founder of an advertising agency, and you want to attract some all-star talent. You're looking to expand your content marketing department, and you really want content marketing experts to reach out and apply to work for your company.

What most agencies do is the following:

- **The agency posts on social media (Facebook, Instagram, LinkedIn, etc.),** "Come join our amazing family!" Since this is essentially an advertisement, nobody engages with it, which means the algorithms don't feed it to more people, which means nobody sees it.

- **The agency then writes up a job description.** They go around and post this to as many job boards and websites as possible, but new applicants continue to be lackluster and stale.

- **The agency then gets frustrated and decides to hire a PR firm.** They instruct the PR firm to find a columnist to write about the amazing culture the agency has—and how content marketing experts should apply. Again, this is an uphill battle because most columnists know readers don't wake up in the morning excited to read an advertisement about how great an agency's culture is. And when the PR firm does finally find a columnist to write a piece about them, the article gets less than 1,000 views. Nobody cares.

As a result, hiring remains difficult for the agency—and a significant amount of time, energy, and resources have been spent in the process.

The Golden Intersection is the answer to all of these problems.

Let's say I'm the agency owner.

Instead of trying to promote myself and my agency, I should be thinking about what questions my target reader is actively asking themselves. What are their wants, needs, and desires? And how can I make them "the main character" in my story?

If I want to hire content marketing experts, then my target reader is someone who is very knowledgeable about content marketing *and* someone who is looking for a certain type of work environment.

Here are a few examples of pieces I could write to attract those types of readers:

- 6 Tools Every Content Marketer Needs To Be Using In 2020 To Drive More Exposure, Convert More Customers, And Be 10x More Productive

- 3 Reasons Why Every Digital Marketing Agency Should Have Their Own Internal Content Marketing Department

- Are You A Freelance Content Marketer? Here Are 9 Clever Ways To Find More Clients

As a content marketer, these are the types of pieces you are most likely reading on a regular basis. Your *desires* are to make more money, have more freedom, work with better clients, improve your skills, etc. Which means, if these are the types of readers you want to reach, then these are the questions you need to be answering *for the reader's benefit.*

Now let's say you decide to write the piece, "6 Tools Every Content Marketer Needs To Be Using In 2020 To Drive More Exposure, Convert More Customers, And Be 10x More Productive."

In the third or fourth Main Point of the piece, you can say:

> *"The best content marketers are obsessive about using data to measure success. One of the things we do internally here at Digital Press is hold weekly workshops where our team of content marketers will pull up that month's search volume for each client, and then brainstorm growth hacks we can all use to drive exposure. This helps team members not feel like they're "on an island" and solely responsible for finding all the answers themselves, while simultaneously being able to continue learning new skills and mastering the craft of content marketing. For example, some of the growth hacks that have come out of these sessions have been...".*

It's very subtle, but in this example I am speaking directly to the wants and needs of a lonely but talented content marketer who wants a job that will provide him or her opportunities to continue learning. I don't need to spend an entire piece talking about my agency. In fact, doing so would yield 10x less viewership. It's much more effective to casually mention a benefit relevant to the reader in a sentence or two as context to whatever it is I'm explaining.

Again, by talking about yourself "less," viewership goes up—because I'm not making the piece about me, I'm making it about you, the reader.

The Art of Conversation

The advanced version of The Golden Intersection is what's commonly referred to as "The Humble Brag."

If you've ever been to a fancy dinner party before, then you know exactly what this sounds like. It's the subtle turn of phrase an individual uses when they want to draw attention to something *without making it seem like they're drawing attention to it at all.* It usually sounds like this:

"That's a great point. So I actually own a design firm over on Sunset Boulevard—for context, we design clothes for Kanye West, Beyoncé, Travis Scott, basically the who's who in the entertainment industry—and one of the big things we've learned about design trends is…".

Listen closely, and in these conversations you will actually hear people say the words, "for context." They are using their own accomplishments and achievements as credibility for whatever it is they're talking about. When done tastefully, this can be a powerful strategy to give people just enough information to pique their interest. But when done repeatedly, this becomes a neon sign that all you care about is talking about yourself.

To execute this masterfully, here are some rules to follow:

- **Always bring things back to the reader's wants, needs, and desires.** At no point should your story or "for context" information *equal or exceed* the amount of time you spend talking about the reader. The vast majority of everything you write should be directed to answering your target reader's questions, or giving them valuable insight that will move them one (or many) steps forward in the direction of their own goals. One or two sentences about yourself is usually plenty. Remember: less is more.

- **Only mention information that is truly relevant to the topic at hand.** If you're talking about content marketing, don't plug your sales tool just because. If you're talking about growing vegetables at home, don't promote your friend's vegan cookbook. If you're talking about clothing design, don't randomly say to your readers, "Which is why I've chosen to partner with Fiverr, for all your design needs." The only time you should be "promoting" something—whether it's yourself, your company, or a specific product—is when that thing gives appropriate context to the topic.

- **Make the thing you want to draw attention to part of a larger point.** You should never dedicate an entire section, no matter how big or small, to your own self-promotion. It's far more effective to embed the thing you want to draw attention to within a thought, Main Point, or insight. For example, instead of dedicating an entire paragraph to your new book, mention your book within a statement directed at the reader's benefit. Say something like, "I tell the story in full in my memoir, *Confessions of a Teenage Gamer*, but one of the first lessons I learned was...".

- **Use casual language.** You want any and all self-promotion to sound like part of the story you're telling. 99% of people who work in PR make this mistake by saying somewhere in the piece, "Enter: <Company Name>." They literally introduce the thing they're trying to promote with a massive spotlight— which immediately makes the reader feel like they're being sold to, and no longer the center of attention or "main character" of the piece. Instead, be more subtle. Use casual language like, "I originally told this story in my book," or, "Before I started my first company, Digital Press...". Self-promotion should never feel like self-promotion. It should feel like context. That's it.

- **Make whatever it is you're promoting "the setting" for the story.** If you're writing a piece about workplace habits, you have the opportunity to promote your own company's workplace by making it *the example* of whatever insight you're sharing with the reader. You can say, "Positive workplace culture is extremely difficult to cultivate, but by practicing these three daily rituals as a team, you'll find it can be nurtured quickly and effectively. For example, every morning at Digital Press, the first thing we do as a team is...". Here,

I'm using my own company as an example of the thing I'm explaining to the reader—not making it the "main character" itself.

The Art of CTAs

A "Call To Action" is a way of directing readers to a specific product, service, or company you want to promote.

The simplest way of executing a CTA is to put it in the signature of the article. Again, at no point in time do you want the reader to feel like they're being sold to, or that they are being treated as the second priority. An easy way of avoiding this issue is to separate the interests of the reader (the piece itself) and your own by placing any links or sales pitches at the very end of the piece.

For example, once I had started building an audience for myself on Quora, I wanted to direct those readers to my website (to capture their email addresses) and my company website (to attract new clients). So, at the end of all my articles, I linked to both a valuable resource for target readers, as well as the Digital Press website. My signature looked like this:

> *Thanks for reading! :)*
>
> *Want to learn how I built my Personal Brand online, attracting over 50 million readers?*
>
> *Click here to take the free Personal Branding email course!*
>
> *Want to work with Digital Press? Check us out!*

By placing this signature at the end of every article, I was able to give readers the *option* of clicking elsewhere if they wanted to, without making them feel taken advantage of or "sold to" within the article itself.

This is one way of executing a CTA.

A better, less obvious strategy for inserting a Call To Action into a piece is to make the CTA a credible example of whatever it is you're talking about.

For example, let's say you're writing a piece about personal branding, and you want to send people to your "Free Personal Branding Email Course."

Instead of placing this CTA in the signature of your article, you can embed the link inside a relevant paragraph. In one of your Main Points, you can say something like, "Personal branding can be a difficult marketing strategy for people to execute on their own. I have been helping people build their personal brands online for more than five years now, and more than 10,000 people have taken my *free personal branding email course (link),* explaining step-by-step what goes into building a personal brand on the internet.

Here, the CTA and "credibility statement" are being combined into one.

This is a great way of drawing attention to something you want a reader to know about, without making it the focal point of the piece. If the reader is interested in a free personal branding email course, they'll click. And if they're not, their eyes will just skim right over it and continue reading.

No harm done.

The final way of executing a Call To Action, without ruining the reading experience, is to link to your website, company, or product without any overt explanation.

For example, instead of actually saying, "I have been helping people build their personal brands online for more than five years now, and more than 10,000 people have taken my *free personal branding email course (link)*," you would instead just say, "I have been helping people build their personal brands online for more than five years now," and link the phrase, "...helping people build their personal brands online" to your free personal branding email course.

What you're doing here is associating a specific phrase within a sentence to whatever asset or product you want people to know about. Here, the words in the sentence actually say "helping people," so when paired with a link, it's safe to say a reader will think to themselves, "Well, I'm looking for help—I wonder where this goes." Instead of calling out your product or service directly, you're letting the reader discover it on their own.

My personal preference when it comes to CTAs is to always make them feel like helpful and relevant resources for the reader, but to never give them the spotlight. Very little is gained by trying to hard-sell readers on anything. Instead, it's far better to not try to sell them at all, and to just make whatever it is you *do* want to promote easily accessible.

If the reader wants what you have to offer, trust they'll take it upon themselves to navigate there on their own.

And if they don't, let them continue reading in peace.

Otherwise they won't want to read any more of your material.

Chapter 10

Your Content Roadmap: Constructing A "Sticky Web" For Your Writing

Anyone can follow all these rules and write one really great article.

The real question is, can you write 1,000 of them?

Writers who succeed on the internet are the ones with the largest libraries of content. Sure, there are outliers who happen to find success with just a small batch of material, but 99% of the time, volume is what separates "good" from "great." The more material you have, the more times you're "spinning the wheel" of social algorithms, and the more likely new readers are to discover you and your work.

In the game of Online Writing, **volume wins.**

Every time you write something online, your footprint gets bigger.

The more material you write within a given category, the more dominant your voice becomes.

And the longer you stick with it, new writers *in your chosen category* will start to compare themselves to you.

How?

The first way is to take a *timely* approach.

Timely writers write about what's happening *right now*. These are *BuzzFeed* writers chasing the next pop culture trend, *Wall Street Journal* columnists chasing the next viral news story, and people on social media adding commentary to today's hot topics.

The beauty of timely content is that it has a much higher likelihood of catching fire immediately—simply because you're riding the wave of mass attention. When I wrote for *Inc Magazine,* some of my most-popular articles piggy-backed on events happening in the news: Mark Zuckerberg making an announcement, the Golden State Warriors winning a championship, etc. Since search volume and social media engagement around those topics was high, those pieces received a disproportionate amount of attention in the short term.

Unfortunately, timely content is a double-edged sword.

If you think of your writing over the span of 10 years (opposed to 10 days), these timely pieces have a very short shelf life. It wouldn't make sense for me to re-publish or re-share my article about an announcement Mark Zuckerberg made seven years ago. I would need to do a considerable amount of re-writing in order to make that "same article" relevant today—and in most cases, I'd be better off just writing something new.

In this sense, only writing timely material makes it difficult to build a library of content that lasts.

The second way to think about writing online is to take a *timeless* approach.

These are stories, opinions, insights, lists, and guides that will stand the test of time. They could be read today, or they could be re-read ten years from now, and they would still remain valuable to the reader. The principles are universal.

Of course, not everything you write will remain a "perfect" reflection of how you think or feel over the long term. For example, some of the things I wrote in 2014, 2015, and 2016, I no longer agree with—or would explain differently today. And that's OK. Because for every piece where that's the case, there are ten more I re-read and think to myself, "Wow, I completely forgot I worded it this way—this is great." What's important is that I, as the writer, have the option of making that decision for myself (opposed to the decision being made for me simply because a topic is no longer relevant).

Timeless content very rarely commands the same level of hype that a trendy, hyper-relevant, timely piece receives in the moment. It's hard to compete against something the entire country, or even the entire world is fixated on for 24-48 hours. However, where timeless content "wins" is in its ability to endure. A timely article might accumulate 10,000 views in a day, and then fade into the abyss—whereas a timeless article might accumulate 5,000 views every year for ten years.

And I much prefer the latter.

The reason timeless content is a better long-term investment is because you can continue to reuse, re-publish, and re-share this content long into the future. The more you write, the bigger your library of *usable* content grows. The more your library grows, the larger of a footprint you can now bring to any new writing platform. The larger of a footprint you can bring to new platforms, the faster you will effectively position yourself as "the king" *of your chosen category*—and over time, this flywheel will continue to spin faster and faster.

For example, one of the reasons I was able to grow so quickly on Medium was because I already had 2,000+ usable articles in my library of content.

I didn't start writing on Medium until 2017. By then, there were already millions and millions of writers on the platform (admittedly, I joined the game a bit late). However, I had been writing daily on Quora for almost three years, and had amassed a library of content at my disposal. So, I started taking all my old material and republishing it on Medium, one article per day. Between 2017 and 2020, I wrote less than 30 original pieces on Medium. All of it was previous material from my library, just with a new title and a new picture—and in my first year on the platform, I accumulated tens of thousands of followers, millions of views, and became a Top Writer in more than 15 different categories.

All from old material.

Now, had I been exclusively writing *timely* content on Quora, I wouldn't have been able to do that. Nobody on Medium would have wanted to read opinion articles about news events that happened two years in the past. The value of my library came from the fact that 99% of it was timeless—in the sense that I could re-publish the same article three years later, and it would still read the same way, and still provide relevant value. This is what I like to call "earning dividends" on content you created historically.

So, in the game of online writing, it's not just that volume wins.

It's that *timeless* volume wins.

Content Buckets

To get the most "return on investment" from your writing, it's important to have a roadmap for success.

I firmly believe the first six months on the internet, for any writer, should be spent exploring, practicing, and gathering data. Even for our clients at Digital Press, we would explain that the first three months were largely about gathering data. We'd then author a handful of pieces with them in a variety of categories, and as data told us what people were engaging with, we would narrow down their topic areas to clearly define their three "content buckets."

The three types of "content buckets" I recommend are:

1. **General Audience:** You should have one bucket that is aimed at universal topics. Things like positive habits, life lessons, productivity topics, etc., are big, broad categories that resonate with the widest number of people. How you make them relevant to you is by approaching them through your own specific lens. Let's say you're the VP of

Marketing at a software company. You should write about life lessons learned *as the VP of Marketing at a software company*, or time management techniques you use day in and day out *as The VP of Marketing at a software company*. This same logic applies no matter who you are. You could be a poet, a foodie, or a master salesman, and there is still massive benefit in targeting universal topics through your own specific lens.

2. **Niche Audience:** Your second content bucket should be hyper-relevant to your expertise. If you're the VP of Marketing, then your niche audience would be "marketers"—and refined further, maybe "content marketers." When speaking to this audience, you have the option of continuing to leverage universal topics to broaden your reach, or intentionally excluding general audiences by speaking directly to the intimate pain points your target reader is experiencing. My recommendation is to do both.

3. **Company/Industry Audience:** Your third content bucket is the environment and industry you exist within. If you're a violinist, you should be writing about the violin industry. If you're a music producer, you should be writing about the music production industry. If you own a SaaS business, you should be writing about software as a service and the SaaS industry at large. If you are a writer, you should be writing about writing (in your spe-

cific genre). This third bucket is usually the easiest to pinpoint, however it's an important one to add into the mix in order to be "seen" as a leader *in your chosen category*.

For example, here are my three content buckets:

1. **General Audience:** Life advice, personal development, and self-mastery as it relates to my own life experiences as a writer and entrepreneur (and previously as a body-builder and professional gamer).

2. **Niche Audience:** Online writing advice, self-publishing, and content marketing.

3. **Company/Industry Audience:** Thought leadership and personal branding, specifically for executives, founders, investors, etc.

Now, it's important to remember that your content buckets can, and most likely will change over time. When I first started writing on Quora, I experimented with a ton of different Niche Audiences before data told me what people really wanted to hear about from me most. I wrote about gaming, I wrote about bodybuilding, I wrote about big brand advertising campaigns, etc. Eventually, I learned it was really my perspectives on writing and content marketing that attracted the most consistent attention as a "niche," so I doubled down on that.

Endless Idea Generator

Anyone who says, "I don't have that much to say," doesn't know the secret to coming up with endless ideas.

Writing anything on the internet follows a very simple 3-step process.

Step 1: What "Type" Of Writing Is This?

    Form #1: Actionable Guide

    Form #2: Opinion

    Form #3: Curated List

    Form #4: Story

    Form #5: Credible Talking Head

Step 2: What "Idea" Am I Communicating Within This Piece Of Writing?

    Idea #1: Explanation (When/Where/How/What/ Why Something Happens)

    Idea #2: Habits (To Achieve A Destination, Goal, Or State Of Being)

    Idea #3: Mistakes (Keeping You From Achieving A Destination, Goal, Or State Of Being)

    Idea #4: Lessons (Learned In Pursuit Of A Destination, Goal, Or State Of Being)

    Idea #5: Tips (That Can Help You In Your Own Pursuit Of A Destination, Goal, Or State Of Being)

Idea #6: Stories (That Symbolize Or Explain Some Aspect Of The Pursuit Of A Destination, Goal, Or State Of Being)

Idea #7: Timely Events (That Are Relevant To The Target Reader's Knowledge, Awareness, Or Pursuit Of A Destination, Goal, Or State Of Being)

If you notice, timely "this just happened" content is only one of seven types of ideas that are communicated in written content—and yet, writers disproportionately give them priority in their libraries. Instead, I recommend you give timely content the smallest allocation of your writing portfolio. Take advantage of opportunities when they present themselves, but invest the majority of your time in building timeless assets you will be able to repurpose and reuse (and will pay you dividends) years into the future.

Step 3: Why Me?

Credibility #1: "I am an expert on this topic. Here's what I think."

Credibility #2: "I went out and talked to all the trusted experts on this topic. Here are all their insights and opinions in one place."

Credibility #3: "I'm just sharing my opinion, but my opinion is the most articulate one of all."

When you combine these three steps together, you suddenly get a very easy (and replicable) equation for consistently writing high-quality, high-performing content.

For example:

- **Curated List x Mistakes x 7 Industry Experts (Credibility #2)** = the outline of an article titled, *"7 Founders Share The Biggest Mistakes They Made Raising Money For Their First Startups"*

- **Credibility x Explanation (Why) x Expert (Credibility #1)** = the outline of an article titled, "I Was A Professional World Of Warcraft Gamer As A Teenager. Here's Why eSports Is Going To Become A Multi-Billion-Dollar Industry"

- **Opinion x Lessons x My Perspective (Credibility #3)** = the outline of an article titled, "Our Country's Economy Is Falling Apart. Here's What That Looks Like For Someone Living In A Low-Income Neighborhood")

Go down the list, combine steps 1, 2, and 3, and you'll have the outline of a piece of content just waiting to be written.

Content Roadmap Template

Once you've pinpointed three content buckets you want to start with, and you've come up with a handful of working headlines using the Endless Idea Generator, you just plug and play to create your Content Roadmap.

Step 1: List Your 3 Content Buckets

Each of these will be the categories you are looking to target over the long term.

- **General Audience** (Example: Productivity)

- **Niche Audience** (Example: Project Management Software)

- **Company/Industry** (Example: Software As A Service)

Step 2: List 3+ Topics Under Each Bucket

Within each bucket, pinpoint a few overarching topics you want to become an "influential voice" on, and write actively about.

- **General Audience** (Example: Productivity)
  - » Productivity Tips
  - » Time Management Techniques
  - » Curated Productivity Insights

- **Niche Audience** (Example: SaaS Startups)
  - » Startup Advice
  - » SaaS Insights
  - » Founder Stories

- **Company/Industry** (Example: Project Management Software)
  - » History Of Project Management Software
  - » Trends In Project Management Software
  - » New Research / Data In Project Management

Step 3: Plug And Play Under Each Topic

Then, underneath each Audience, and then each Topic, use the Endless Idea Generator to come up with hundreds of working headlines.

- **General Audience** (Example: Productivity)
  - » Productivity Tips
    - – HOW TO be more productive
      - · How X Startup Entrepreneurs, Pro Athletes, And Billionaires Stay Productive
      - · How Anyone Can Be More Productive With These X Small Shifts In Their Morning Routine
      - · How To Achieve Work-Life Balance Without Getting Fired
    - – WAYS to be more productive
      - · X Little-Known Ways To Make Yourself More Productive On A Daily Basis
      - · X Unconventional Ways <insert high-profile individual> Stays Productive On A Daily Basis
      - · X Unique Ways To Get More Work Done In 5x Less Time
      - · X Inexpensive Software Products That Will Help You Be More Productive

– THOUGHT LEADER RECOMMENDATIONS
  on how to be more productive

  · What Michael Jordan's Training Sched-
    ule Can Teach Us About Productivity

  · Oprah's Morning Routine Will Inspire
    You To Be More Productive. Here It Is

  · These X NYT Best-Selling Books Will
    Change The Way You Think About Pro-
    ductivity Forever

  · These X TED Talks Will Inspire You To
    Scrap Your Current Morning Routine
    And Do Things Differently—Right Now

– BEST BOOKS on how to be more productive

  · This 1 Book On Productivity Will Inspire
    You To Stop Working After 3 p.m.

  · These X books Are Filled With Timeless
    Productivity Hacks Everyone Should
    Read (Or At Least Keep On Their Book-
    shelf)

  · If You Want To Be More Productive, You
    Absolutely Need To Read These X Books
    By The End Of The Year

– PODCASTS to help you be more productive

  · X Podcasts You'll Feel Productive Just
    Listening To

  · X Podcasts That Feature The World's
    Leading Productivity Experts

  · These X Podcasts Will Teach You How

To Simplify Your Life And Be More Productive

- HABITS of highly productive people

  · X Habits Of Highly Productive People

  · X Horrible Habits That Will Keep You From Ever Becoming Your Most Productive Self

  · X Nighttime Habits That Ruin Your Sleep (And Your Productivity The Next Day)

  · X Networking Habits That Will Waste Your Time And Demolish Your Productivity At A Conference

  · These X Habits Might Sound Simple, But They're The Single Best Way To Maximize Your Productivity Forever

- MISTAKES people make when trying to be productive

  · X Mistakes People Make As Soon As They Start A New Routine

  · X Apps People Think Will Make Them More Productive, But Actually Make Their Productivity Worse

  · X Costly Mistakes Every Manager Makes When Trying To Maximize Team Productivity

- MYTHS people listen to (that keep them from being productive)

    - X Things People Think Will Make Them More Productive, But Actually Won't

    - X Productivity Hacks The World Loves To Preach, But Are Just Quick Fixes And Myths

    - X Obstacles Keeping Every Single One Of Us From Moving Productively Toward Our Dreams On A Daily Basis

    - X Types Of Conflict In The Workplace That Eat Up Our Most Productive Hours

- DISTRACTIONS that ruin your productivity

    - X Types Of Distractions That Are Horrible For Productive Work

    - X Distractions That Need To Be Removed From Your Life Before You Start A New Routine

    - X Distractions That Will Kill Your Productivity

    - X Distracting Relationships In Your Life You Probably Don't Realize Are Hurting Your Productivity

    - X Workplace Distractions We Can All Relate To

- **Niche Audience** (Example: SaaS Startups)

  » Startup Advice

    – HOW TO build a startup

      · How To Build A SaaS Company With $0

      · X Ways To Build A SaaS Product Without Raising Any Money

      · There Are X Different Types Of SaaS Startups. Which One Are You Trying To Build?

      · X Key Steps You Need To Take In Order To Build A Successful Startup

    – OPTIMIZING your startup and solving for inefficiencies

      · X Ways To Make The Culture Of Your New Startup More Productive

      · These Are The X Most Common Problems For New Startups. Here's How To Solve Them

      · X Easy Ways To Spot What's Keeping Your Startup From Reaching The Next Level

    – HIRING for your startup

      · X Hiring Mistakes Every Startup Founder Makes Over And Over Again

      · X Hires You Are Going To Need To Make When Your Startup Reaches $1M In Annual Revenue

- These X Hires Will Be Crucial For Your Startup To Scale
- Unless You Hire These X Types Of People, Your Startup Will Never Become Successful
- X SaaS Products That Will Make Your Startup's Hiring Process Faster, Easier, And More Efficient

- SCALING your startup

  - X Obstacles Every Founder Runs Into When Scaling Their First Startup
  - X Ways To Scale Your Startup Without Raising Millions Of Dollars
  - X Scaling Challenges You'll Experience After Crossing $1M In Revenue
  - X Types Of Managers You'll Need In Place Before Your Startup Can Scale Efficiently

- LESSONS you learn building a startup

  - X Unforgettable Lessons You'll Learn Bootstrapping A Startup With $0
  - X Lessons You Have To Learn The Hard Way As A Founder (That You Never, Ever Forget)
  - X Memorable Lessons I Learned Working For An Entrepreneur (Before Becoming A Startup Founder Myself)
  - X Life Lessons You'll Learn About Yourself The Moment You Decide To Start Your Own Company

- HABITS every successful startup should live by

  · X Morning Habits These X Successful Startup Founders Live By (And Have Made Them Millions Of Dollars)

  · If You're Building A Startup, Here Are X Habits You And Your Employees Should Practice On A Daily Basis

  · X Simple But Powerful Habits You Need In Your Life—Especially As A Stressed-Out Startup Founder

- WHY startups fail

  · X Reasons Startups Fail To Raise Their Next Round Of Funding

  · X Painful Reasons Only X% Of Startups Reach Their Series B

  · X Interesting Takeaways From The Harvard Business Review Study That Just Came Out About Startup Failure Rates In America

  · X Crucial Lessons I Learned Watching My First Startup Fail

  · X Little-Known Reasons Startups Fail (That No One Ever Talks About)

- FUNDRAISING for your startup

  · X Simple Ways To Raise Money For Your Next Startup Venture

  · X Ways Founders Are Raising Money

Today, Without Turning To Silicon Valley Angels And Venture Capital Firms

- · X Ways To Raise Money For Your Startup, Even If You Don't Live In A Major City

- · X Powerful Ways To Build An Influential Network And Make The Startup Fundraising Process Easier

- **Company/Industry** (Example: Project Management Software)

    » Project Management Software

    - – TOOLS to improve your company's project management

        - · These X Tools Are Quickly Becoming Essential In The Workplace For Maximum Productivity

        - · X Software Tools That Can Help Your Team Be More Productive

        - · X Pain Points All Remote Teams Face, And X Easy Ways To Solve Them

        - · X SaaS Companies Spearheading A New Way To Think About Workplace Productivity

        - · X Mistakes Companies Make When Looking For An Internal Project Management Software Tool

- WAYS to increase your company's productivity
    - · X Ways To Increase Your Company's Productivity Using Technology
    - · X Ways To Track Employee Productivity Over Time (Without Making Them Manually Log Every Single Task)
    - · X Ways To Help Your Leadership Team Be More Productive Using Software
    - · X Easy Ways To Integrate A SaaS Product Into Your Company's Processes
    - · X Mistakes Companies Make When Trying To Integrate A New SaaS Tool Into Their Culture
- NEW TECH changing the way startups think about productivity
    - · X Software Productivity Tools That Were Ahead Of Their Time
    - · X SaaS Websites You Should Bookmark And Read On A Daily Basis (If You Want To Learn How To Maximize Productivity In The Workplace)
    - · X New Technologies That Are Making It Easier For Startups To Track, Measure, And Scale Employee Productivity
    - · X New Technologies That Are Going To Change The Way Startups Think About Measuring Employee Productivity

- TRENDS in the project management / SaaS space

  · X SaaS Trends That Are Quickly Changing The Way Companies Scale
  · X Productivity Trends That Will Be Ingrained In Every Workplace By 2025
  · X Productivity Trends You Should Live By If You're A Freelancer

- STATS that prove why startups need software to scale employee productivity

  · According To Harvard Business Review, X% Of Startups Now Spend $Y Per Month On SaaS Products Related To Employee Productivity. Here's Why That's Great News
  · This New Study Shows X% Of Employees Want To Measure Their Growth And Productivity Using Their Smartphones
  · X% Of Employees Want To Track Their Own Productivity. Here's How You Can Empower Them To Do So

I know—that's a lot of headlines.

The reason I wanted to actually show you what a Content Roadmap looks like though is so you can see how easy it is to come up with ideas. Using the Endless Idea Generator, you should never run out of things to write about. Ever.

Something else I want to point out is that within this roadmap are some redundancies. Certain ideas could fall under different buckets. Others can exist within two buckets. Etc.

Personally, I don't see this as a bad thing. Part of establishing yourself as an "influential voice" *within your chosen category* is writing at-length about the same handful of topics, and continuing to find new ways to approach them. In this sense, repetition is a good thing—not a bad thing.

Lastly, every time you sit down to write, I encourage you to ask yourself these three questions:

1. "Does this idea fall within one of my three content buckets?" (If not, what can you tweak so that it makes more sense in the context of your library?)

2. "Will this piece stand the test of time?" (If not, what can you change to make it less timely and more timeless?)

3. "Have I already written about this?" (If yes, how can you re-tell those same stories, insights, opinions, etc., in a way that gives the reader a new and different experience?)

I can't tell you how many times I've written the phrase, "When I was 17 years old, I became one of the highest-ranked World of Warcraft players in North America." And yet, every time I've told that story, I've told it through a slightly different lens. In one piece I wrote about how playing video games taught me about work ethic. In another, I wrote about the life lessons I learned being obsessed with something at such an early age. In another, I wrote about the fallacy of achievement, and how external rewards don't last forever. In another, I wrote about my relationship with my parents as a teenager being obsessed with World of Warcraft.

It's the same "story," but told hundreds of different ways.

As a result, "When I was 17 years old, I became one of the highest-ranked World of Warcraft players in North America" became one of my "core narratives." And now, every time I speak on a podcast, or connect with someone new over the internet, this narrative almost always comes up— because people have learned to associate it with me, and me with it.

Remember: repetition is how you reinforce who you are, what you know, and what life experiences are informing your writing, perspective, and unique point of view.

Repetition is how you get people to remember "you."

Chapter 11

Pillar Pieces: How To Turn Proven Online Writing Into Longer, More Valuable Assets

As we talked about at the beginning of this book, your "Writing Data Flywheel" is your mechanism for endless inspiration.

More importantly, your "Writing Data Flywheel" becomes your unfair advantage *within your chosen category.*

The longer you stick with writing online, the more data you will accumulate about what topics resonate with the most people, what headline styles work best for you and your content, what piece structures and styles keep readers engaged the longest, etc. For example, when you see that one of your articles, social media posts, or short stories is outperforming every other piece of content you've ever written, you shouldn't just see that as a "win" and move on. You should question why this piece in particular is resonating with so many people—and how you can expand it into a longer, more valuable asset.

This is the answer to the question, "When should I launch my own website?"

You are ready to launch your own website when you've reached a point where your writing can in some way, shape, or form become a business. Again, 99% of writers and industry leaders want to start here, but it's premature. They end up spending an unnecessary amount of time trying to figure out *how to capture and keep people's attention,* when they could have easily answered that question by Practicing In Public and letting data give them the answer.

Writing becomes a business as soon as you start:

- Capturing people's email addresses
- Making money from advertising revenue
- Making money from paid subscriptions
- Selling products and/or services
- Speaking, coaching, consulting, and/or advising

So if this is the goal, then it makes sense to let data inform where you choose to invest more time, energy, and resources next.

Turning Articles Into Pillar Pieces

It's time to start your own website once you 1) know what it is people want to read about from you, 2) know how you need to position topics to resonate with your target readers, and 3) already have their attention elsewhere and are *ready to move them deeper into your library of content.*

For example, let's say you've written a dozen or so pieces about sales advice, but there was one article in particular about "cold email outreach" that outperformed the rest.

Step one would be to double down on this topic and continue Practicing In Public to make sure this wasn't a fluke. Is there more data confirming that "cold email outreach" is a content bucket that is performing well and resonating with your target readers? If yes, you should refine your original content bucket (Niche Audience: Sales) to be more specific (Niche Audience: Cold Email Outreach For Sales).

Step two begins once you've confirmed these hypotheses. You've written more extensively about "cold email outreach" and sales strategies specific to this target audience, and you've clearly seen this audience is engaging with the insight you're bringing to the table.

You have their attention—now you want to do something with it.

In order to start capturing people's email addresses, or directing them to some sort of paid product, you are going to need to move these readers from whatever platform they're on over to your own website. The difference however, *and why I believe it's so important to first start in social environments,* is now you know exactly how to greet them when they walk through the door. You know your target audience wants to learn more about "cold email outreach" strategies to achieve their sales goals—so you position that, first. Maybe on your website you even say, "Looking for cold email outreach strategies? You've come to the right place." Again, imagine how hard it would be to figure out the best way to "position" yourself without any of this data. You'd be banging your head against your desk, beyond frustrated.

Now, one thing I want to stress here is that just because you have someone's attention on a social platform like Quora, Medium, LinkedIn, etc., doesn't mean they're going to *keep* giving you their attention. In fact, anytime you ask a reader to move from where they already are to somewhere else (especially your own website), you actually have to *work harder* to keep their attention. Every second they spend on your site, they are subconsciously asking themselves, "Why am I still here?"

So, don't just meet their expectations.

Exceed them.

> The best way to continue earning a reader's loyalty is to direct them from a piece of written content they already find valuable, **to a longer, more extensive resource they will want to bookmark forever.**

"Pillar Pieces" are the *most valuable, most comprehensive, most insightful, and most engaging* versions of pieces that have proven themselves elsewhere.

Instead of sending readers from an article on a social platform to the homepage of your website, what you want to do is *exceed* their expectations by giving them a longer, more extensive resource they almost can't believe you're giving away for free. If they thought your articles and written content on social platforms were valuable, they should be blown away by how in-depth your "Pillar Pieces" are on your website. If they enjoyed the short stories you were sharing on Medium or Twitter, they should be amazed you decided to publish what could have easily been an excerpt from a book (or hell, *an entire book*) for free on your blog.

The idea here is to make sure the first interaction a reader has with you *on your own website* is an incredibly positive one. They shouldn't feel like you're tricking them into spending time on your site. Instead, they should feel like you are taking them by the hand and walking them to the *next most valuable, most relevant* piece of writing in your library.

"But Cole, I've already said everything I wanted to say about this topic in the first article I wrote."

No, you haven't.

Here are five easy ways to take a proven topic and expand it into a *timeless* Pillar Piece.

- **Combine Content:** If you've written a dozen articles about "cold email outreach strategies," combine the best parts of them all into one comprehensive guide. Or, if you've written hundreds of tweets about writing advice or cooking advice or fitness advice, you should combine them into a Pillar Piece titled, "100 Tweets That Will Teach You Everything You Need To Know About Cooking Gluten-Free At Home." The benefit here for the reader is convenience. Instead of them having to scroll through three years of tweets, or hundreds and hundreds of Medium articles, you've done them the favor of curating all the best, most relevant pieces of information into one comprehensive piece that lives on your site.

- **Curate Expert Opinions:** It's one thing to share your own opinions and insights, but it's even better if you can reinforce those insights from credible people. Interview experts in your industry and add quotes from them throughout your Pillar Piece.

Pull from interviews they've given on podcasts and in major publications. You can even quote insights they share on their own websites or social content. The more helpful information you can curate, *so long as it's relevant to the reader,* the better.

- **Add Statistics:** Nothing makes a piece feel "more professional" than adding a few highly relevant stats or takeaways from credible studies. You can very easily elongate proven content by adding additional research the reader would have otherwise had to find for themselves.

- **Tell Personal Stories:** If the target range of a piece of written content online is 800 – 1,200 words, then that doesn't leave a lot of room to tell many in-depth stories. The beauty of turning proven material into Pillar Pieces, however, is that you can share much more with the reader—*so long as it's relevant.* In each Main Point, explain to the reader how you learned this same lesson or piece of advice for yourself. Divulge interesting details. Give them the stuff they might not know about you—and wouldn't normally come across in your other content.

- **Provide More Examples:** This book is a great example. One version of this book could have been 800 words. Another version could have been 5,000 words. Another version could have been 25,000 words. The reason why this book ended up being as long as it did was because I wanted to give you (the reader) *a ton* of examples. I didn't just want to explain a point and then move on—I wanted you to see first-hand how these writing strategies worked, so that you could integrate them into your own writing too. The same goes for Pillar Pieces. You can very easily turn an 800-word article into a 5,000 word "Ultimate Guide" by giving the reader dozens of concrete examples.

Notice, I am not encouraging you to inflate the word count and just "make the piece longer."

I'm encouraging you to find ways to make this one individual piece, on one individual topic, as potent as possible.

Once you have a Pillar Piece written on a specific topic, you should then direct readers over and over again to this Pillar Piece in your relevant social content.

This becomes your "Reader Acquisition Flywheel."

- Write content in each of your three Content Buckets.

- Use data to decide which specific topic deserves its own Pillar Piece.

- Create a Pillar Piece on your website.

- Continue to write about that proven topic in social environments, and regularly link to that Pillar Piece in everything you write that is relevant.

For example, let's say you write a Pillar Piece on your website titled, "The Ultimate Guide To Cold Email Outreach: 9 Steps To $100,000 In Monthly Revenue."

Every time you write about "cold email outreach" (speaking to your Niche Audience) on social platforms like Twitter, Quora, Medium, LinkedIn, etc., you now have the option of elegantly directing readers to your website *without making them feel sold to.*

This goes back to "the art of talking about yourself without talking about yourself."

You could write a Medium article titled, "3 Mistakes Most Freelancers Make Using Cold Email Outreach To Get New Clients," and within one of the Main Points of the article say, *"Another one of the mistakes I see freelancers make is they treat cold email outreach the same way they treat emailing their friends and family members. They don't write with the person they're trying to reach in mind. For example, I know many freelancers who try to target C-level executives with cold email, but end up sending them 500+ word emails. This is a big mistake, because most CEOs don't have the time to read 50-word emails, let alone 500-word emails. I explain why super short emails are far more effective in my* **ultimate guide to cold email outreach,** *but the important thing I want you to remember is that brevity is key."*

Then, you could write another, different article on LinkedIn titled, "Why Cold Email Outreach Is The Single Most

Effective B2B Sales Strategy In 2020," and within one of the Main Points of the piece say, *"Anyone not using cold email outreach in 2020 is massively disadvantaged. At the beginning of the year, I published a resource on my site, **"The Ultimate Guide To Cold Email Outreach: 9 Steps To $100,000 In Monthly Revenue,"** and in that guide I explained how companies with cold email strategies outperformed companies without cold email strategies.*

And so on.

By connecting Pillar Pieces to your Content Buckets, you will eventually have hundreds and hundreds of content pieces pointing to your website in a way that is non-intrusive for the reader. Instead, readers will feel like they just stumbled onto a goldmine—first, discovering one of your pieces in a social environment, and then within that piece, discovering an *even more valuable, even more relevant* piece of writing.

This is how your library of content starts to become a super-sticky web.

Turning Pillar Pieces Into Email Courses, Newsletters, And Free Downloads

Once you have readers on your site, now it's time to capture their email addresses.

The same way you want to turn proven articles into Pillar Pieces, you also want to turn proven articles and Pillar Pieces into longer, more valuable resources and products. Again, instead of "wondering" what you should create next, let data tell you. If you're seeing one Pillar Piece is getting significantly more traffic than the others, you should consider turning that in-depth piece into an even longer, even more valuable downloadable PDF worksheet or guide, or even a 7-day email course for beginners, etc.

The idea here is to never make the reader feel like they're being presented with something "out of context."

What you want to do is build a road for them to follow:

- They click on an article that speaks to their interests

- Within that article, they see a link to a more valuable resource that speaks to their interests

- Within that Pillar Piece, they are presented with *an even more valuable resource* that speaks to their interests

- And so on

Unfortunately, most writers (including the content writers and marketers within multi-billion-dollar companies) aren't this thoughtful with their readers and customers. Instead, they badger them with advertising that says, "Sign up for our newsletter!" or "Click here to download our FREE report!" What they fail to realize, however, is that readers don't just "sign up" for things. Readers don't just give away their email addresses and long-term loyalty because you presented them with an offer ("Join my newsletter for more of my thoughts!"). The same way people make judgements about what to read on the internet, they also make (even harsher) judgements about what to opt-in for on someone's website—which means your offer has to be even *more relevant, and even more valuable* than all the written content they've consumed of yours thus far.

How most writers go about solving for this is by withholding their best content.

"Well, if my goal is to capture email addresses and make money, then I should only give away a little bit of my writing for free. I should make them have to download or pay for the rest."

As a result, their writing in social environments never catches on (because it's all fluff masked as a sales pitch), which means their Pillar Pieces never get any traffic (because nobody is reading their social content in the first place), which means nobody ends up opting-in or purchasing anything on their site. Frustrated, they throw their hands in the air and say, "Writing on the internet is broken. It doesn't work." And then, if they're a company or wealthy individual, they go hire an agency that specializes in Facebook Ads so they can throw money at the problem.

Again, I encourage you to flip the script.

Give away 99% of your best writing **for free.**

Play the long game. Become the most-read, most-valuable writer *in your chosen category.* Your goal should be for readers to tag you on Twitter and say, "I seriously can't believe all this amazing content is free." Your only problem should be *having too much of people's attention,* and not having enough hours in the day to capture it all. That's far better than not being able to get people's attention in the first place.

So, if you've already written hundreds of articles on a given topic, and you've already created a handful of insanely valuable Pillar Pieces on your site, how do you keep pushing yourself to create even more valuable, even more relevant resources readers can download or opt-in and receive?

In addition to the ways I mentioned earlier (turning articles into Pillar Pieces), here are a few more:

- **Speak To 1 Hyper-Specific Problem:** Just like articles, the best email captures speak to highly sensitive issues within readers. For example, if you write often about building your real estate portfolio, you could create a 7-day email course titled, "7 Days To Buying Your First Rental Property." Even though readers have consumed your other content, this feels like a hyper-specific solution to a problem they're facing ("How do I buy my VERY FIRST rental property?")— and the idea of being walked through the process over 7 days feels helpful.

- **Curate Credible Case Studies:** Another proven opt-in format is to create your own case studies of well-known success stories in your industry. For example, let's say you are a fiction writer, but you also write articles (and have a handful of Pillar Pieces) about how to earn a living as a fiction writer. You could create a downloadable PDF titled, "10 Fiction Writers Who Earn $100,000+ Per Year By Self-Publishing On Amazon." Now you have

a list of fiction writers who are not only interested in more of your "How To Write Fiction"
content, but may also be interested in reading
your own works of fiction as well.

- **Early/Exclusive Content:** Can you capture
  email addresses as a storyteller? You bet.
  Allow readers to download the first chapter
  of your upcoming (not-yet-released) novel
  in advance. Or, allow readers to opt-in for
  access to additional storylines and side
  plots of the main characters from your
  books. Whatever it is, just make sure it is
  specific enough for the reader to imagine
  what they're going to be receiving in return
  for giving away their email address. Saying,
  "Subscribe for more of my writing!" isn't
  enough.

- **Different Levels Of Audience:** As you
  learn more and more about your readers,
  you can (and should) create resources for
  each level of reader. For example, if you are
  a digital marketer and you regularly write
  about digital marketing strategies, all your
  readers aren't going to fit within the same
  bucket. You're going to want to create one
  free email course for beginners ("Getting
  Started: 5 Days To Setting Up Your First
  Profitable Facebook Ad"), another free email
  course for advanced marketers ("30 Days, 30
  Examples Of How To Maximize Facebook Ad
  Revenue And Convert 10x More Leads Into
  Customers"), and another free email course

for experts ("7 Days To $1 Million: Facebook Ad Strategies For Experts").

- **Templates/Worksheets:** Readers love things that are "plug and play." For example, if you write about health and fitness, you can allow readers to download a handful of specialized workout routines. Or, if you're a memoir writer, you can give readers on your website a template for them to write a memoir of their own. Or, if you're a leadership coach, you can give readers a worksheet for them to facilitate their own team-building exercises at work.

For example, one of the first opt-ins I ever created on my site was an email course for people looking to build their personal brand online.

I had been writing about personal branding on Quora, as well as *Inc Magazine*, and those pieces always got a high level of engagement. People would email me asking how I built my personal brand, and how they should get started building their own. So, I combined a handful of my most popular articles into a 7-day email course titled, "7 Steps To Start Building Your Personal Brand," and hosted it on my website.

Data told me this was a resource my readers wanted—and that email course has since captured tens of thousands of email addresses.

Turning Articles/Pillar Pieces/Email Courses/Newsletters Into Products & Services

You've been writing online for 6-12 months...

You've learned what readers want to hear about from you (through data), and you've clarified your Content Buckets...

You've launched your own website, and written a handful of Pillar Pieces...

You've created a few *even more relevant, even more valuable* resources for readers to opt-in and download...

Now it's time to sell them something.

But first, I want to pause.

Do you see how linear this path is? Could you imagine how many unanswered questions you would still have if you had started out, *day one*, trying to write and sell a book, or a product, or a course? Do you understand how acquiring data about your readers seems like the longer road, but in reality, it's actually a shortcut?

One of the most legendary copywriters in the world, and a great friend and mentor of mine, Craig Clemens, summarizes this point perfectly. "People don't buy products. They buy solutions to *urgent* problems." Most writers who try to enter the game and write a book, or expect their first article on the internet to be a viral sensation, think they know what their target readers' urgent problem is—but they don't. They are assuming. They are guessing. They have zero proof that they clearly understand the intricacies of the problem. And furthermore, they have not yet proven that *the market has determined them the best possible source of information for that particular problem.*

(This is true for both fiction and nonfiction by the way.)

As a result, they put in all this hard work and effort, only to launch their book, or paid newsletter, or course, or whatever, only for it to fall on deaf ears.

They didn't know how to speak to their target reader.

As a result, their target reader didn't listen.

When you give 99% of your "best stuff" away for free, that means you should only monetize the last 1%. **And in that last 1% should be just as much, if not EVEN MORE value than the other 99%.**

I am not exaggerating when I say I have probably written more than 1,000 articles on the internet just on the topic of writing online.

I have written about it on Quora and Medium. I have created Pillar Pieces and downloadable resources on my website. I have spoken on podcasts. I have held workshops and presented at masterminds and conferences. Almost every single piece of insight in this book, I have shared somewhere else already for free.

So then why did you buy this book?

- **Convenience:** You didn't want to go scrolling through my library of 3,000+ articles to find the ones about writing. Buying this book and having all those insights here was easier (I saved you time).

- **Specificity:** You didn't want to piece together handfuls of takeaways from all my free content. You wanted an entire resource dedicated to one specific topic: how to write online.

- **Depth:** You didn't just want to read an 800-word article on the topic of online writing that barely skimmed the surface. You wanted 200+ pages, and you wanted examples, and you wanted stories, and you wanted to feel like if you went down this rabbit hole and made it all the way through this book, you'd emerge 100x more knowledgeable and prepared for success.

It's the same reason Digital Press became a million-dollar business in less than 10 months, and a multi-million-dollar business in less than 2 years.

I have written hundreds of articles on the internet about personal branding, and how to position yourself on the internet as a leader in your industry. The answers on how to do it are out there for anyone and everyone to use for themselves. The problem is, founders of companies, C-level executives, investors, international speakers, those types of people don't have the time to learn and master those skills for themselves—nor do they have the time or expertise to effectively share their thoughts and insights at scale on the internet.

So what do they do?

They hire someone—*specifically, someone who actively writes about the very thing they want for themselves.*

The best products and services are a reflection of your proven, high-performing topics.

If readers are devouring your written content about how to write a memoir, why not turn "Memoir Coaching" into a business?

If readers are hooked on your short stories about what it's like working as a developer at Facebook, why not turn that into a paid newsletter?

If readers are loving your opinion articles about brand messaging, why not offer "Brand Messaging" as a service for companies?

> The art of online writing is all about letting readers tell you what it is they want more of, **and what they're willing to pay for.**

Then, once you've effectively captured and held their attention, you can present them with the *next most relevant, most valuable* piece of content in your library.

This is how you (finally) make money as a writer.

Chapter 12

How To Make Money Online As A Writer

This is the question every aspiring writer asks first.

Which is why I'm answering it last.

Making money as a writer shouldn't even be on your list of priorities until you've proven the following:

- **You can (and want to) write IN PUBLIC on a regular basis.** 1x per month is barely cutting it. 2x per month, OK. 4x per month, now you're getting somewhere. DAILY? Shoot me an email (cole@nicolascole.com), because I want to invest in YOU.

- **You have clearly defined your Content Buckets.** You know what your high-performing topics are. You know how to capture and keep your target readers' attention. You've learned (through trial and error) what they like, don't like, and want more of.

- **You have launched your own website and positioned yourself in your niche.** You know (through data) what your most valuable content is. You have planted your flag in the ground and said, "This is who I am. This is what I write about. And if this is what you're looking for, you've come to the right place."

If you've put in the work and gone through these steps, then guess what?

Now it's time to make some money.

There are only 3 ways to monetize your writing: Ads, Paywalls, or Services.

Let's break them down.

The Advertising Model

AKA: "The Attention Model."

The first route to profitability as a writer is to generate enough "attention" for you to go out and sell that attention to someone (usually a company or brand) that wants to reach your target audience. For example, most YouTubers make money by running relevant pre-roll ads on their videos. Most Instagrammers make money by taking a picture with a product and promoting it to their followers. Most high-traffic bloggers make money by running Google Ads on their website. All of these are different examples of the same model: attention in exchange for dollars.

The problem, however, is that in order for this model to generate any money at all, you need a shit-ton of attention.

For example, when I wrote for *Inc Magazine*, I made money through the advertising model.

As a publication, *Inc* brings in about 20 million page views per month. All that "attention" is valuable, and can be sold to companies looking to target *Inc*'s readers (small business owners, entrepreneurs, managers, etc.). How *Inc* makes money, as a business, is they go out and sell banner ads on their site to companies looking to target those same customer demographics—and then display those ads on the articles I (and every other columnist) write for the publication. When someone reads one of my articles, *Inc* makes money, and in turn, I make money. (For context: I made a penny per page view. So even with millions of views on my work, I wasn't exactly going yacht shopping.)

While the advertising model might seem great, it has a handful of flaws:

1. **People hate ads.** If you've ever tried reading an article on *Inc* or *Forbes* or any other major publication, you've experienced the 10-second seizure your computer goes into before letting you scroll down the page. Then, as soon as you start to scroll, a Kia video ad takes over your screen. This is bad for reader loyalty—and why social environments are much more beneficial for building audiences.

2. **People don't trust dozens of different sponsorships.** If you see an Instagrammer promoting a different product every other week, you're going to eventually stop taking them seriously. But in order to maintain consistent revenue, you need to constantly be partnering with brands. Over time, because you are promoting different products, people start to see you as "fake." This same logic applies to writers. If you are constantly promoting different products in your articles or writing, eventually readers are going to feel

like the attention they're giving you is being taken for granted.

3. **Ads require a ton of volume.** Very few writers for major publications get paid, simply because they don't bring in enough traffic to warrant adding them into the business's payroll system (their monthly checks would be the equivalent of a cup of coffee). In order to make any real money, whether you're a writer for a publication or you have your own website and are running your own ads via Google, you need to be accumulating hundreds of thousands of page views every month to even break $1,000. And if $1,000 sounds like a lot of money to you, go write 30+ articles in a month and track your hours. When all is said and done, you're effectively earning well below minimum wage.

4. **Ads are volatile.** Some months writing for *Inc*, I made $3,000. Other months, I made $400. When you are making money purely off "attention," revenue goes up and down based on performance—which makes it very hard to make forward-thinking decisions. In fact, the biggest reason why I waited so long to quit my 9-5 job (even though I was out-earning myself writing for *Inc*) was because my money was dependent upon me going viral. I didn't feel comfortable giving up my full-time salary until I had months and months of data showing me what I could consistently generate from a revenue per-

spective, on average.

The reason the advertising model is so popular, however, is because it's also the easiest model for people to understand—which is why so many people pursue it.

Unfortunately (or maybe fortunately), no social platform has successfully monetized "attention" for writers the way YouTube monetizes attention for video creators. Medium was trying to, but their model has since shifted to the "paywall" model.

As a result, many writers continue to write online with no real awareness around how to turn page views into dollars.

Here's how you can monetize your writing with the advertising model:

Sell Ad Space Within Your Content

The same way major publications go out and sell ad space to big brands and companies, you can do the same thing within your written content. A few years ago, when Medium was pushing their "publications" run by community members (anyone could start their own publication and recruit other writers on Medium to contribute pieces), this was how nearly every single publication was monetized. Someone (like you or me) would start a publication around a topic (say Life Advice or Startup News), recruit dozens and dozens of writers to contribute pieces, and then go out and sell sponsorships and ads within the articles that appeared on that publication.

You can do the exact same thing as an independent writer.

If you have a big enough audience (minimum 5,000-10,000 followers), and you are attracting enough traffic (minimum 50,000 – 100,000 page views per month), you can reach out to brands looking to target the same audience as your readers, and see if they'd be willing to advertise on a few of your posts. They'd essentially pay you to link to their site, or one of their resources, somewhere within those pieces. Do note, however, many brands that do this also request a pretty heavy-handed "sales pitch" for their company (and you need to educate them on why this is a terrible idea), requiring you to write something like, "Which is why I recommend XYZ Company, the best-tasting, most affordable product I've ever experienced!"

When selling ad space, you're either going to make money selling:

1. **Impressions:** How many people "see" the post.

2. **Clicks:** How many people click the link to the brand's website/resource/etc.

3. **Conversions:** How many people see, then click, then actually convert into a lead (email address) or customer (successful purchase) for the brand.

If this seems like a lot of work with a steep learning curve, that's because it *is*.

You're now a full-time writer *and* ad-selling specialist.

> **Note: You can only do this on social platforms. On major publications, as soon as a piece is published, technically they "own it." They also*

have pretty strict clauses in their contracts
that say columnists cannot receive payment in
exchange for mentioning or promoting another
company, product, service, etc.

Land A Brand Sponsorship

A slightly easier way of executing the above is to just
partner with one brand exclusively in some sort of formal
capacity.

This is extremely common in other industries—Michael
Jordan sponsored by Nike, for example—and yet it is
almost nonexistent in the world of publishing. Personally,
I believe as more and more writers realize the power of
social media, and are forced to build their own audiences,
brand sponsorships between companies and writers will
become more common.

How writers monetize at the brand level today is by selling
banner ads somewhere on their website. A fitness writer
will let a supplement company "sponsor" their site for a
month—putting their logo and some product shots on a
header on their site. Or a music blogger will let a music
label "sponsor" their blog by putting pictures of their artists' albums and songs all over the place.

Brand sponsorships typically last about a month, and then
based on the performance of the campaign (again: impressions, clicks, conversions), the brand will decide whether
or not they want to continue sponsoring you and your
site. If your website is doing millions of page views, this
can be a lucrative path to monetization. But again, you
are responsible for finding the brands. You're responsible

for "selling" them on why their advertising dollars should be spent sponsoring your site (for example: you have an insane amount of traffic, or you have a hardcore, super-engaged reader base, etc.). And you're responsible for all the invoicing and accounting.

My honest opinion here is, by the time you build a website bringing in millions of page views, you're most likely going to learn there are far better (and much easier) ways to make money as a writer.

Run Google Ads On Your Site

The most common way writers (specifically bloggers) make money online is they build up traffic on their website and then integrate Google Ads to make money "passively."

Individual sites do this. Publications do this. The whole idea behind Google Ads is to "turn them on" and then allow their advertising network to run ads on your site that relate to your audience. The pro here is that you don't really have to manage anything—you don't have to go out and find the brands willing to spend money on advertising, you don't have to negotiate any of the deals, etc. But the pro is also the con. Since it's all "plug and play," you don't have too much say over what ads appear on your site (they will be loosely related to your target readers though) and can very quickly make your site look like a cheap destination.

Personally, I am not a big fan of this path to profitability.

Think of ads as a lever. In order to make more money, you need to run more ads. But the more ads you run, the less space on your site is actually dedicated to your writing—which destroys the quality of experience for your readers.

However, you need your readers to keep coming back in order to show them ads, in order to make more money.

It becomes a bit of a vicious cycle where you either decide you don't care at all about the reading experience to maximize earnings, or you maintain a positive reading experience but end up not making enough off ads to warrant even running them in the first place.

Become An Affiliate

Affiliate marketing is an extremely popular way of making money as a content writer.

All "affiliate marketing" means is that you make commission on every sale you facilitate. For example, if you have a large audience of readers interested in direct response marketing, you could become an affiliate for Clickfunnels (a company that sells software for direct response marketers). Then, every time you write a piece about direct response marketing, you could (elegantly) say in one of your Main Points, *"...and if you're looking to build your own marketing funnels, I recommend taking a look at a company like Clickfunnels."* You would sign up as an affiliate for Clickfunnels, generate your own unique link, and direct readers to their website via your link and make a commission if they become a customer.

Another popular example of affiliate marketing is with Amazon.

If your audience is interested in mystery stories, you can become an affiliate with Amazon (anyone can sign up to do this) and use your affiliate link every time you recommend a new mystery story to your readers. When they click and buy the book on Amazon, you receive a commission. As a best practice, most writers disclose to their audiences who they are an affiliate for and why ("Full disclosure: This is an affiliate link."), but as long as you're recommending relevant products to your audience, most readers don't mind.

While this might sound like small potatoes, it's worth pointing out that affiliate marketing is a $7 billion-dollar industry. I know writers who make six-figure incomes purely off (elegant) affiliate marketing woven into their writing. But this is also a monetization path that is typically better suited for digital marketers and content writers than essayists, novelists, self-help writers, etc., although I have seen it executed in those categories as well.

Done tastefully, affiliate marketing can be a great second or third revenue stream for you to add into your portfolio.

Don't Monetize Your Writing—Monetize Your Personality

The last way you can (technically) monetize your writing is by leveraging other social platforms with advertising models.

Instead of trying to make money off the attention of your writing, you can direct that attention to your YouTube channel, or your podcast, or your Instagram page, where you *talk* about writing, or *share tutorial videos* about writing, or *post pictures* of you traveling the world as a writer, etc. We are living in an age where sometimes the best path to making a living "doing what you love" is finding creative ways to monetize not necessarily the craft itself, but all the things that surround the craft: *how you write, where you write, who you write with and learn from, your knowledge about writing, etc.* You might discover you can make far more money as a YouTuber making writing tutorials than you ever could writing.

However, this usually requires you to "shift" your dream.

For many years, I fought myself on exploring these other paths of monetization. Some part of me felt like I was "giving up" on the dream of being a full-time, professional writer and author if I made any money whatsoever doing anything except writing. What I ended up realizing is that even when you do start making money off your writing, you're still going to want to diversify your income streams. What happens when your best-selling book stops selling? What happens when your website traffic starts falling? What happens when you decide you want to pivot to a new genre, or add a completely different "content bucket" into the mix? Do you really want to go back to being a barista (or in my case, a copywriter at an advertising agency) and start from ground zero all over again?

My recommendation is to explore anything and every-thing that advances your writing career forward, and can "double" as a marketing vehicle for your writing, allowing you to add more revenue streams into the mix.

And that means monetizing more than just your writing.

The Paywall Model

AKA: "The Exclusivity Model."

The second route to profitability as a writer is to charge for access to your content.

The paywall model is essentially the opposite of the advertising model. Where the advertising model requires a massive following in order to start monetizing, the paywall model can begin day one (although I still recommend going through the steps in this book, otherwise you're going to make some pretty big assumptions about what people are willing to pay for).

For example, the first money I made "as a writer" was by selling my fitness eBook series on my website in 2015.

While my answer to the Quora question, "Is it possible to change so much you no longer recognize yourself?" was going viral, I realized I could monetize the attention I was capturing by selling "access" to a *more valuable, more relevant resource*. Instead of going out and trying to sell that attention to a brand or company, I decided to monetize it myself by creating my own product and putting it up for sale. The 1 million views I accumulated on Quora made me $0 through the advertising model (because Quora doesn't reward writers with money in exchange for viewership), but made me thousands of dollars through the exclusivity model (charging for access to the eBook on my website). I added a link to my two eBooks inside the post, and a percentage of readers (who wanted to know my workout routines and meal plan) clicked and bought my products.

Now, you do need some sort of "attention" in order to

monetize "exclusive" content—however the barrier to entry is much, much lower. With the advertising model, you need hundreds of thousands of page views in order to even make a few hundred bucks per month. But with 1,000 loyal fans and readers, you can start generating serious revenue through the paywall model. I highly recommend reading the essay "1,000 True Fans" by Kevin Kelly, where he explains how you really don't need millions of readers in order to make an amazing living as a writer. Instead, if you can get 1,000 true fans (who spend at least $100 per year buying and supporting everything you put out into the world), you can earn yourself $100,000 per year.

That is a completely attainable and realistic goal for any writer.

I much prefer the "exclusivity" model to the "attention" model, but here are a few of the challenges that come with monetizing access:

1. **You still need to build "attention" in order to start monetizing.** It doesn't need to be a massive audience, but it needs to be an audience nonetheless. So while a lot of writers want to skip to the part in the story where they launch a $20 book and start cashing checks, the truth is, you still need to go through the steps. You still need to gather data from your readers. You still need to nail down your Content Buckets. You still need to successfully move them from free social environments over to your website. And you still need to gain clarity around what problem you're actually solving—and what your

target readers will be willing to pay for. The only difference here is that you can begin this process with a niche audience of 1,000 followers.

2. **Your "exclusive" content needs to be even better than your free content.** Making really great free content is hard (much harder than people realize). But making paid content is even harder—and yet, most writers have them flipped. They think anyone can write free content on the internet, and the only respectable form of writing is the kind you get paid for. I wholeheartedly disagree. If you can't write free things on the internet that capture and keep people's attention, chances are, you aren't ready to release a paid project. Of course, there are the success stories (one in a billion) that prove otherwise, but I don't find "playing the lottery" to be a very strategic life decision.

3. **Paid content requires a higher level of attention to detail.** The advertising model has caused massive issues within our society (a topic for another time), primarily because it encourages the wrong behavior. It's a model that rewards quantity over quality, and where "visibility" tends to trump "ability." As a result, creators just sort of "spray and pray." They pump out as much content as possible with the hopes of capturing eyeballs and increasing ad revenue. Paid content, on the other hand, incentivizes loyalty. If you

are paying for access to something—especially on any sort of month-to-month basis—you have very high expectations as a consumer. You expect good quality. You expect a positive experience. You expect the product to be delivered on time, in a professional manner. There is more "at stake." As a result, writers who successfully monetize with paid content tend to make far more money—but also have to spend far more time creating products people love buying again and again.

My personal belief is that the "exclusivity" model is the future for writers in the digital age. We are moving into a world where, because of the internet, we don't need to be heard by millions of people in order to make an impact. Instead, we can create and discover niche communities that are hyper-specific to our interests—and in some cases, we're even willing to pay for access.

Here's how you can monetize your writing with the exclusivity model:

Write Behind A Paywall

More and more websites today are forgoing the advertising model to build subscription revenue instead.

If you've noticed, publications like the *New York Times, Wall Street Journal,* etc., have started putting their content behind a paywall. They might give you three free articles as a taste of what you can expect, but after those three articles you're required to pay in order to keep reading. Sites like

Medium and Wattpad are also exploring this model, requiring readers to pay per month for access to their content, and then compensating writers for regularly publishing exclusive content for the site to monetize in the first place.

As a writer, part of making money off your craft means constantly keeping your finger on the pulse of what new platforms are emerging for you to leverage (and if you want to be the first to know what those opportunities are, then I highly recommend subscribing to my paid newsletter—SEE HOW THIS WORKS????).

For example, Wattpad recently launched Paid Stories. The way they describe it on their website, "Wattpad Paid Stories is our response to readers who want the opportunity to show support for the writers they love. Writers can now earn money for their work on Wattpad from readers who appreciate it." How it works is readers buy "coins" within the platform/app, and then use those coins to unlock chapters or entire stories from their favorite writers.

When I first found out about Wattpad's Paid Stories though, I realized this feature was only available for the highest performing writers on the platform. Which meant, in order for me to use this mechanism to monetize my own writing, I would need to publish a ton of free content on Wattpad (and stick with it for at least six months, to learn *through data* whether or not Wattpad's audience actually found my writing valuable) to build myself up on the platform. If I invested a year or two, maybe I could unlock this feature for myself as well.

Does that mean other writers shouldn't try to monetize on Wattpad?

Not at all.

But knowing what would be required in order to make it financially successful is an important piece of the puzzle.

Create A Product

It took me a very long time as a writer to realize when you're writing a book you ultimately want to sell, you're doing much more than just *writing*.

You're trying to sell a product.

When a customer looks at a $15 package of words, what drives their decision to purchase is not the fact that you took the time to write the thing in the first place. What drives their purchase is *what they believe your words can do for them*. Sometimes, readers buy books because they speak to their *wants, needs, and desires*. Other times, readers buy books because of what the author stands for, or the controversy surrounding their story. And every once in a while, readers buy books because of the cover, which they believe will add a great accent color to their coffee table.

Regardless, the *customer* is buying a *product*.

Now, writing a book is one way to make money as a writer—but if you notice, it's one of many. A product could also be a workbook, a calendar, a coffee mug, a leather-bound journal, a t-shirt, a candle, or a deck of cards with inspirational phrases from timeless writers. Ryan Holiday, best-selling author of "The Obstacle Is The Way" and "The Daily Stoic" is a great example. After "The Daily Stoic" became a best-selling book, he realized (through data) his readers wanted more information about stoicism. So he launched dailystoic.com, where he now sells memento mori medallions, rings, pendants, "The Daily Stoic Challenge" deck of cards, and even a 5.5" hand-sculpted pewter portrait of Marcus Aurelius.

Sell A Course

While writing a book might seem like the most "literary" way to make money, it's usually not the fastest (or most profitable) path to earning a living as a writer. For context, in order to make $1 million dollars as a writer, you need 100,000 people to buy your $10 book.

Or, you need 5,000 people to buy a $200 course.

These are different paths, requiring different skill sets, however there's no reason why they can't work in concert with each other to provide you (the writer) with more financial upside and long-term security.

James Clear, the author of "Atomic Habits," one of the best-selling self-help books of the past few years, is a perfect example. On his website he has a $299 video course called "The Habits Academy," which is him, sitting in front of his bookshelf, essentially walking listeners through the same information that's already in his book—just in video form. So, why have thousands of people signed up and purchased this course? Maybe because they don't like reading, but love watching videos. Or maybe they are huge fans of James Clear and want as much access to him and his knowledge as they can get (remember: 1,000 true fans). Or maybe it's because the video course offers a bit more structure and account-ability—and if someone is struggling to build positive habits, they're willing to make a $299 investment in themselves.

The reason why Clear and other best-selling authors are now launching courses is because even *they* know how difficult it can be to earn a great living purely off book sales. Mark Manson, author of the best-selling book, "The Subtle Art of Not Giving A F*ck," is another example. He sells six different life advice courses on his site.

When you launch a course, your readers then become more than just fans of your books.

They become leads for you to convert into higher-ticket customers.

Start A Paid Newsletter

This is my new favorite way to monetize as a writer.

Think of paid newsletters as micro-paywalls. Instead of building yourself up on a platform with a paywall like Medium or Wattpad, you can start a paid newsletter on Substack and start monetizing your "exclusive content" there instead.

The reason why I believe paid newsletters are going to be the future for writers is because they provide monthly subscription revenue. For example, I have no idea how much I'm going to earn every month on Medium. It's the same problem I had when writing for *Inc*, where my earnings were tied to performance. When one of my articles goes viral, I make great money. When I go a month or two without a viral hit, my income drops.

The difference with paid newsletters is that readers have to subscribe on a monthly basis. This gives you (the writer) more stability and reassurance that your income isn't going to just magically disappear 30 days from now. You can also begin monetizing with this path much faster than you could building yourself up on a platform like Medium. 1,000 true fans at $10 per month is $10,000 every 30 days. That's a six-figure income by serving a very small, very niche, very loyal audience.

Don't make it more complicated than it is: a paid newsletter is nothing more than *an even more relevant, even more valuable* part of your library. For example, you could take your book-in-progress and publish it chapter by chapter as a weekly paid newsletter instead of publishing it the conventional way—and probably make more money.

Who says a book needs to be "a book" anymore?

Host A Workshop/Event

Lastly, you can hold a workshop, event, panel, curated discussion, or "class," where you share additional information with your tight-knit community.

Think of this as a more meaningful way for you to engage with your audience, fans, followers, and readers. It's one thing to read someone's insights online, or in a book, or even hear it from them in a pre-recorded video course. But it's a very different experience getting to be in the same room as that person, or connect with them live in a virtual setting.

When curating an event, just think about what additional value you can provide your readers. If you're a fiction writer, host a fiction writing workshop, or an event where readers can help you brainstorm storylines for the characters in your next book. If you're a non-fiction writer, consider creating an online class where you help other writers learn how to outline, title, and self-publish a memoir. If you're a copywriter, put together a panel of copywriters who have generated tens of millions, even billions of dollars in sales, and make it an exclusive experience for ten aspiring copywriters, $250 per seat. If you're a blogger, put together a mastermind group that meets once per month to share strategies for increasing website traffic.

Personally, I love hosting virtual workshops—and I do often with writers who are subscribed to my newsletter. When I studied fiction writing in college, the focal point of the program was to bring your writing to class that week and read it aloud to the semi-circle of twelve or so students sitting around you. I quickly realized how fast I was growing as a writer by having to say my words out loud, forcing me to hear unnecessary words or sections that dragged on and on. When I started Digital Press, I used this same workshop technique with every single writer and editor we hired, reading client pieces aloud over Zoom and asking the group, "What did you notice? What stands out to you in this section?"

Being able to facilitate these types of experiences is a skill in itself—and one you can certainly charge for.

The Services Model

AKA: "The "I'll-Do-It-For-You Model."

The third and final route to profitability as a writer is to do for others what you've already (successfully) done for yourself.

If you know how to write viral content, people will pay you to write viral content for them.

If you know how to write thoughtful, articulate opinion columns, people will pay you to write thoughtful, articulate opinion columns for them.

If you know how to write high-performing email courses, PDF guides, whitepapers, etc., companies and solopreneurs will pay you to create those same assets for their company.

If you know how to write (and market) a book to #1 on Amazon, people will pay you to help them write (and market) a #1 best-selling book on Amazon.

Basically, anything you know how to do, *with an end result that other people want as well,* can be sold as a service.

Unfortunately, most writers aren't aware of the value of their own skills. To be honest, most people in life don't know the value of their own skills. We all exist in our own little bubble, and get so used to the things we do and know, that we don't even stop to consider how these skills or insights could be valuable for someone else. Since it's "common knowledge" to us, we assume it's "common knowledge" to everyone else—when that couldn't be further from the truth.

Here's how you can monetize your writing with the services model:

Content Writing

The term "content writing" is all encompassing.

Companies need content. Founders and business owners

and entrepreneurs need content. Influencers need content. Celebrities need content. Authors need content. Investors need content. Websites need content. Universities need content.

The list goes on and on.

The internet is nothing more than one massive library of content. In order for us to communicate with each other, we need things to read, watch, listen to, consume, and share. That means essentially every single entity with a presence on the internet, in some sort of capacity, needs content—and if you can provide the words they need, then you're in demand.

That said, the biggest mistake "content writers" make, as well as the companies who hire them, is thinking their job is to write words. And it's not.

Most content writing jobs hyper-focus on word count. "We need several 500-word blog posts," or, "We need a 3,000-word Whitepaper." But all words are not created equally.

Here, let me show you.

> **Example 1:** Most content writing jobs hyper-focus on word count.

> **Example 2:** Giraffes eat purple but sunshine is the reason.

Both these sentences have eight words. Are they both valuable to you, the reader?

No.

Writers who price their value based on the number of words they write are 1) implicitly saying "all writers are created equal so just find the cheapest option," and 2) are working toward the wrong goal. The goal is not to write a 500-word blog post, or a 3,000-word Whitepaper.

The goal is to write something that is *even more valuable, and even more relevant* to the target reader—and successfully encourages them to take some form of action (sign up for a newsletter, purchase a product, etc.).

If you can deliver this sort of result, you will have no problem earning a living as a writer.

Ghostwriting & Speechwriting

Think of ghostwriting as luxury content writing.

If content writing is primarily for companies, then ghostwriting is for the people who run and represent those companies (and/or any other public personality).

I fell into the world of executive ghostwriting when I was 26 years old. No one told me this industry existed. None of my teachers in college ever mentioned it as an option. What happened was, a very successful entrepreneur who had previously sold his company for north of a billion dollars, sent me an email. He was an avid reader of my *Inc Magazine* column, and was wondering if I would be willing to help him share his stories and insights as an entrepreneur as well.

One client turned to two.

Two turned to four.

And a year later, Digital Press employed more than a dozen writers and editors, and we had more than 50 clients all around the world.

Now, there are some stigmas that surround the world of ghostwriting. Some people refuse to let someone else "write" for them—which is fine, they aren't your ideal client. And many writers refuse to lend their pen to someone else. Personally, I don't see ghostwriting this way. I see it much closer to co-writing, in the sense that I could be the most talented writer on the planet, but I don't have the insights, the stories, or the palette of colors to write whatever is being shared with me in conversation from someone much more experienced and further along in their career.

It might be my pen, but it's unquestionably their thoughts, ideas, and perspectives.

The reason ghostwriting is such a viable path for writers is because, for one, you essentially get paid to build an immensely valuable network. Second, ghostwriting is far more lucrative than conventional content marketing. You have to remember, you aren't selling "words on a page." What you're selling is clarity of a message—and so how much is it worth, to that particular person, for them to communicate clearly?

Third, ghostwriting requires you to learn how to write in a wide variety of voices. Writing for a male executive is different than writing for a female executive. Writing from an investor's point of view is different than writing for a founder. Writing for a musician is different than writing for a professional athlete is different than writing for a politician.

Being able to learn how to weave in and out of all these different types of voices will only make your own writing better.

Copywriting

Most people don't actually know what the term "copywriting" means.

Casually, people use the term to imply just about any sort of business writing: website copy, landing page copy, email copy, ad copy, etc. But the truth is, the art of copywriting goes so much deeper than that. I've spent time around some of the most financially successful copywriters in the world, and I can tell you they spend as much time obsessing over which words will trigger the right emotions in their target readers as Dostoevsky probably spent refining *Crime & Punishment.*

Copywriting is a very unique skill—and one that requires a considerable amount of time to master.

However, the reason why I consider it such a viable and worthwhile career path for writers (regardless of whether your dream is to become a full-time fiction novelist or a best-selling self-help author), is because copywriting teaches you how to *sell*. Whether we realize it or not, we as writers are "selling" readers our ideas. This entire book is dedicated to "selling" you on the idea that you should write online. When you read *Harry Potter*, J.K. Rowling is "selling" you on Hogwarts and Quidditch and all the things that make Harry's world real. When you read anything, you are being sold an idea—and depending on how much those ideas resonate with you determines whether or not you continue reading, as well as whether or not you decide to tell five of your friends what you've just read.

Copywriting is arguably *the* most lucrative career path for writers, specifically because top-notch copywriters get paid to drive a financial result—of which they reap part of the upside. For example, it's common for world-class sales copywriters to get paid six figures to write a single sales letter. And if that sales letter can successfully convert leads into profitable customers, the copywriter can share in the profit (usually amounting to hundreds of thousands, if not millions of dollars).

Company Messaging, Consulting & Advising

"Messaging" is writing at the corporate level.

When you get good enough at understanding how words can shape people's perceptions, thoughts, emotions, and reasons for action, you become much more than just a writer.

Companies all over the world are constantly asking themselves, "How can we better communicate who we are? How can we speak to our customers in a way that's different from the competition? How can we educate the world on this new problem we're looking to solve?" Very few writers realize they can utilize their linguistic talents in this domain—and it's a shame, because it pays exceedingly well.

This typically ends up falling under the umbrella of "consulting and advising."

At the end of the day, people will always pay for expertise. The writing, publishing, and media landscape has so many different avenues that if you can master any single path, you will become an incredibly valuable source of information for anyone headed in that direction. If you've mastered the art of keyword hacking on Amazon, you can position yourself as the go-to resource for that information. If you've mastered the art of writing high-performing Facebook ads, you can build an entire business around doing nothing except writing Facebook ads for companies. If you've mastered self-publishing niche fiction, you can consult major publishing houses on how to get with the times and bring more readers to their own fiction authors. If you've mastered writing pitch decks that allow companies to raise millions of dollars in funding, you can get paid to tell startups what changes they need to make in their messaging to attract the attention of investors.

The more time you invest in your skills as a writer, and the more you continue to expand your portfolio of revenue streams by combining any of the above, the more money you will make—and more importantly, the more time you will have to reinvest in the writing you enjoy doing the most.

Final Thoughts

If you want to become a successful, professional writer today, you have to become more than just a writer.

You have to also be an entrepreneur.

The pipedream that a publishing house is just going to swoop in, save the day, and bring you tea and crumpets all afternoon while you stare out the window working on the next great American novel is dead. It doesn't exist. Hemingway had a good run, but as soon as the internet was invented, that era came to an end.

Today, the writers who succeed, *and who actually make money*, are more than just writers. They are brands. They are solo-run companies. They are the publisher, the creative director, the distributor, and the writer, all wrapped up into one—and they embrace the additional responsibility, because it means they have more monetary ownership and creative control over their work.

Instead of shying away from this new world, and wishing things were different, I encourage you to welcome it with open arms.

Either way, this is the direction the publishing world is headed.

So as my 8th grade math teacher used to say, "You can either get on the bus, or you can get off of the bus. Either way, we're leaving."

Chapter 13

The 1 Habit Every Single Writer Needs To Master In Order To Become Successful

Most people who read this book aren't going to implement any of the information shared here (hopefully you're not one of them).

And the reason is because, *the real issue*, the "root of the root" that keeps talented writers from ever making their dream come true has nothing to do with writing.

It has to do with discipline.

It has to do with self-belief.

It has to do with understanding the path of mastery.

I know for a fact that everything I've shared with you in this book works. I know because I've lived it. I know because in order to test my theories, I've taken these formulas to my closest friends and encouraged them to execute—and they have achieved similar results. I know because those friends all accumulated hundreds of thousands, millions, even tens of millions of views on their work, had pieces republished in major publications, and had some sort of "event" happen as a result of their writing (invited to speak on a podcast, connected with someone they wanted to connect with, leveled-up their professional perception, etc.). I know because I then built a company around my formulas, and worked with more than 300 different entrepreneurs, executives, investors, speakers, Grammy-winning musicians, Olympic athletes, and *NYT* best-selling authors—publishing thousands of articles, accumulating millions of views, building social followings, launching books and other products, and consulting for some of the largest, most successful companies in the world.

All of these outcomes came as a result of one very clear, very simple habit.

Writing—a lot.

One of the most common questions I get asked from writers is, "How do I get views on my articles? How do I get published?" There's a sort of entitlement in their voice as they say it: "I *deserve* to be read. I *deserve* to be a published, financially successful author—so tell me, how does it happen?" What they fail to realize, however, is that none of their actions, none of their habits, none of their efforts warrant the outcome they desire for themselves and their writing. They treat it as a hobby. They do it on the weekends. They don't invest any time in learning how to market themselves as a writer, or the business of writing, and they don't sit down, day after day after day, and *just write.*

Instead, they think about writing—and hope that'll be enough.

All growing up, my dad used to wear this raggy old no-sleeved shirt whenever he would lift weights in the basement. On the back was a silhouette of a basketball player, and over it was a long paragraph. In that paragraph, it said something to the effect of, "Somewhere, someone else is practicing harder than you, faster than you, longer than you. They want it more than you. And when you meet them, they will win"—with the Nike swoosh as the period at the end.

Writing online is a game. Publishing, and becoming a best-selling author, is a game. Content writing is a game. Ghostwriting is a game. Consulting and advising companies on their messaging, and writing a fiction series that becomes a movie that then becomes a line of action figures co-owned by Disney, these are all games.

Anyone can play the game. And anyone can master the game.

The question is, do your habits reflect your desires?

Do you truly deserve to win?

Nicolas Cole is an author, viral writer & ghostwriter, and founder of Digital Press and Different Publishing.

He is best known for his conversational style of writing and has accumulated more than 100 million views to date.

Cole rose to internet stardom in 2015 when he became the #1 most-read writer on Quora, accumulating tens of millions of views on his viral articles about personal development. His work has been republished in *TIME, Forbes, Fortune, Business Insider, CNBC, The Chicago Tribune*, and many more of the internet's most popular publications.

In 2016, Cole became one of *Inc Magazine*'s Top 10 contributing writers, accumulating millions of views on his business & creativity column, and in 2017 he founded a ghostwriting and thought leadership agency called Digital Press, writing on behalf of more than 300 Silicon Valley founders, company executives, venture capitalists, Grammy-winning musicians, Olympians, NYT best-selling authors, international public speakers, and more.

Today, in addition to regularly authoring new books and articles online, Cole also publishes a weekly paid newsletter sharing insights into both the art and business of becoming a writer in the digital age.

You can subscribe here: https://howiwrotethis.substack.com/

He currently lives in Los Angeles, but will forever be from Chicago.

Made in the USA
Columbia, SC
29 January 2021

31791723R00187